THE W[illegible]ARD

Nature's Principles and Practices for Empowered Living

A practical, radical, and innovative new way of thinking, living and being, for total harmony with oneself and with life.

ISHMAEL TETTEH

Acknowledgement

We pay the price when we go against the tides of nature. Mankind lives by many principles which are non-workable because they are not in harmony with nature. I count myself very blessed to be the channel through which the materials in this book are made available to the world.

This book would not have been possible without the aid of these great disciples and friends:

Mrs. Esta Tetteh, Rev. Doreene Hamilton, Kathy Juline, and my secretary Efua Kumwaa Mensah, who worked beyond her normal hours to make this printing possible.

Special thanks also go to my dear wife, Mrs. Joan Tetteh, for her unfailing support and inspiration.

Contents

Foreword

It was nearly thirteen years ago on an African pilgrimage that I first encountered the teachings of Brother Ishmael Tetteh. I had no previous knowledge of this African mystic when, together with others in my group, I walked through the doors of the Etherean Mission. I shall never forget what happened next. Just as I took my seat in the circle, he directed his gaze penetratingly upon me and asked, "Are you the one?" Without hesitation I responded, "Yes," astonishing myself and those in my party. For approximately the next twenty minutes Bro. Tetteh began asking me questions about spiritual principles. Apparently pleased with my responses, he thunderously announced, "He's here!" I looked back towards the entrance expecting to see a respected tribal elder, but no one new had entered. Addressing my quizzical look, Brother Tetteh gently explained that in 1986 he and some of his students went to the equator to vision and pray for a teacher from the West who would be of support to his movement in Accra-North, Ghana. I was that teacher. (Synchronistically, it was in 1986 that I was visioning and praying with my close circle of spiritual seekers about founding a spiritual community in Southern California.)

He continued teaching, saying, "You are a mystery and a wonderment of God that is constantly unfolding. You conspired with Life to be here at this time and in the manner which you came. You are a mystery to be explored." While these were not new spiritual concepts to me, never did I expect to hear about self-directed spirituality in the depths of Christian Africa. Even more astonishing was how nearly every word that followed so closely resembled my talks to the community I founded in Los Angeles, California, the Agape International Spiritual Center. I wondered if it were possible that somehow an Agape member had given a taped talk of mine to Brother Tetteh. This was not a mental accusation of imitation, and I meant no arrogance; it was simply my mind's attempt to unravel the synchronicity of events that got me to his village, to his spiritual community, to his message of individual wholeness and universal oneness with the human family.

Today, after thirteen years of meditating and praying together, teaching together, and visiting each others' spiritual communities, I can confidently say that it is one thing to hear a person's message, it is quite another to know that person's heart, the birthplace of his wisdom and compassion that become his offering to the world.

And now you, the person holding *The Way Forward*, may enter the depths of self-exploration Brother Tetteh teaches. On the pages that follow you will learn how to become intimately self-acquainted, how to intuit your life's purpose, what you have come to create and share with the world. You will discover if your core philosophy has been formed by your own life's journey, or if it remains one formed by societal influences—familial, educational, religious and cultural. Most importantly, you will learn how to hear and speak with your own authentic voice.

Brother Tetteh's wisdom-teachings will support you in untying the knots of doubt, fear, worry and misunderstanding that bind you. As you attune yourself to the evolutionary impulse governing the universe, you will begin to glow with insights, blessings and benedictions. Expect a deep-down involution, and an introduction to your next level of evolution. Above all, celebrate with great joy the journey homeward within.

Michael Bernard Beckwith, Founder, Agape Int'l Spiritual Center

The Way Forward

A Dynamic Book for Motivation, Wisdom, and Personal Growth

"Man must overcome deeply embedded false concepts to live a fully empowered life." *Brother Ishmael Tetteh*

This book provides you with:

An insightful philosophy for living a life of personal freedom.

The vision to recognize erroneous thinking that keeps you a prisoner to an unrealized life.

Techniques to gently free you from pain and activate your full potential.

Principles that can form the bedrock of your personal philosophy, enabling you to live a life that reflects the highest and best you are here to be.

Introduction

Deep within every person is the desire for peace and for a life that serves their individual highest good and the highest good of all mankind. From the dawn of man, through the centuries to our present time, this desire remains unfulfilled. The simple reason is that mankind lives with and by principles and philosophies that are not in harmony with nature. Well phrased words and semantically rhyming philosophies are not enough to produce the inner satisfaction we call peace. Any life principle, however beautifully it is crafted, will work only if it is in harmony with nature. When we go against nature, we pay the price; and nature is too huge and vast to be circumscribed by our thoughts and human principles. If we want peace, we must ask life.

What is peace? How do we define the essence of this quality? If you were to ask many different people to tell you what peace is, they would most likely tell you what peace is not rather than what peace is. They may, for example, tell you that 'peace is not the absence of war.' This is not a true definition. Such a definition still fails to arrive at the truth of what peace really is and what it means in our lives. It was important to me to capture the true essence of this powerful word. By researching into life and dialoguing with the people of great intelligence in the universe who are concerned about our evolution, I came up with this definition for peace. "Peace is the identification and free expression of our inner potentialities." I have discussed this definition in principle 17 of this book so I will not go into details here. I want, however, to draw your attention to the fine details we need to understand in order to experience what we desire.

This book challenges the popular thinking patterns that keep humanity in mental and emotional slavery. It stimulates thinking towards man's personal and spiritual freedom. It opens the reader to a new paradigm of freedom. It provides a personal fine-tuning based on the working nature of spirit and intelligent evolution.

You will learn that what you *are* is more important than what you *have*, because what you are is eternal. When you give attention to what you are, you discover you are in life to have it all and use all of it to expand what you are. You know what to shift to reclaim your freedom. You can become truly unhindered by realizing that your prison is your own creation. You are meant to be a free spiritual being, respecting others for what they are and celebrating one another in passionate bliss.

You do not need a lifetime or many lifetimes to experience enlightenment. Reading and practicing the principles here will lift you into instant joy and provide you with the vision of possibilities and the route to it.

This work is a great gift. It is not averse to any teaching, yet it challenges and enhances all teaching. It provides the missing link for understanding and appreciating life. It shows what is needed for the advancement of every social and spiritual teaching, and provides practical means for the rapid fulfillment of the goals they seek to achieve. The principles are simple but they evoke passionate joy in all who study and practice them.

Just reading the materials will transform you. If you feel shocked while studying the chapters, be delighted, for the text is either triggering a past mental or emotional picture of pain and removing it or activating a hidden ability and enhancing it.

Read on! Each principle will become a scepter of light, striking hard at fear, anger, apathy, and spiritual confusions, and calling forth your highest good into manifestation.

Many blessings,

Brother Ishmael

The Core Philosophy

From individuals to groups to entire communities and extending throughout the world, we are driven by our core philosophies.

A core philosophy is the central belief and knowledge system that drives your life. You think and act from and through the energy field of your core philosophy. It is responsible for your thoughts, emotions and attitudes as well as for your responses to what happens to you. It is your center and default. It is the generator of your life story. It is what runs your life. It is your identity, your persona, your sense of self and who you are at your deepest level. It is what protects you, shapes your vision and predetermines where and what you will be throughout your life journey.

If we are to effect lasting change in our lives, it is vital that we not only understand what core philosophies are and how they shape our lives but also how we can permanently and finally change them to suit our highest vision for our lives. This book shows the way forward to achieving this.

If your core philosophy or that of the society you live in is wrong, everything you or the society you live will ultimately be wrong. Your best efforts will only give you temporary palliative comfort. Have you ever felt inspired by a motivational speaker or a great book and yet could not achieve what it prescribed? Have you ever said to yourself, now I'm really going to improve my life, only to find that within a few days you're back to your "old" self? This is so, because you will always default back into your core philosophy. It is your soul's residence.

Certainly, compared to the days when we lived in the jungle with our animal cousins, we have made progress in social uprightness. We have learned some social politeness that inspires us to say "please," "excuse me" and "thank you." Most of the time, however, these are routines only.

If we were to ask ourselves what the most important things in life are, we would find that the answer is universal. The core desire of every person is peace, happiness, and love. In an attempt to provide these, we have developed wonders of technology and science; yet the sorrows deepen and the human fears and frustrations have become epidemic. If we do not address our most fundamental nature, we are doomed to repeat our mistakes throughout eternity. Yet if we can grasp the essence of who we are and live in harmony with nature, we can finally transcend our humanness and live a life of utter joy, peace, and bliss.

You might naturally ask yourself, "So how do I get there?" You may have already tried numerous programs, including books and self help gurus that promised to change your life. The truth is that any meaningful program that will transform your life and society must address your core philosophies – the philosophy that drives your life. Whether you will experience heaven or hell is determined by the core philosophies you live by. If you agree with me that so far, the core philosophy humanity has lived in has not provided the needed peace and happiness desired by all, then we are ready to move forward into lasting change.

This book is about changing the core philosophies of life. The tools provided are the easiest for decoding the code of your nonworking core philosophies, and providing you with the tools to quickly embrace philosophies that work.

To be workable, every philosophy and the principles that go along with it must be in harmony with nature. Nature starts from the electron, neutrons and protons of the atom and extends to the infinite galaxies. It is too complex to be circumscribed by your mind and human efforts. To go against nature is to pay the price for it. An easier way of living is to live by "Nature's Sense." You must step down from technology sense into common sense then upscale into Nature Sense. It is easy to do.

Whether your life is meaningful, substantial or successful depends on your Core Philosophy. It predetermines your interpretations and expectations and if they are not in harmony with nature you will hurt and injure your life. For the majority, your Core Philosophies are not in harmony with nature; they are passed along to you and you have just accepted them.

The human paradigm has so far not worked, and there is nothing to suggest that it will ever work, because its current principles are not in harmony with nature. I invite you to read on with an open mind and integrate these principles into your daily life. My promise to you is that if you embrace these fundamental principles, your life will change for the better and you will experience miracles in your every day life. Enjoy your new journey.

Brother Ishmael Tetteh

"I am a universal citizen; I come from Africa and nature is my teacher."

How to Use This Book

The principles in this book result from many decades of spiritual research on what keeps humans away from the attainment of their highest good. Each principle is capable of setting you free. Some of the principles directly address the "cuds" that run your life while others address the need to reinforce and expand "soul abilities."

At the end of each principle, a program for release and empowerment is provided. Use the prompts and processes to release yourself from [1]cuds or to reinforce and expand your identified soul [2]ability.

Where a program for release is not available, use one of the three master programs in the appendix. These programs relate to every principle and may be used in addition to those provided. Use them to process yourself to empowerment.

---

[1] The mental and emotional picture of pain with all the perceptions of the five senses.

[2] This refers to the infinite God potential in man.

PRINCIPLE 1
The Principle of Existence

Life is about pain, but pain is not about you.

There are two forces for existence; they are the forces of pain and pleasure. By pain, I mean the mental, emotional and physical obstacles and injuries such as physical diseases and accidents, emotional upsets, fears and guilt, and mental anxieties and worries. Its opposite, pleasure, is the success, joy and happiness we feel when all is going well.

The thinking system of mankind is that life is for pleasure and pain is an enemy. You are directly or indirectly taught how to resist or escape from pain. This thinking system is so strong that it created a so-called devil as the cause of your pains and hell as the home or the final residence of perpetual pain. Primarily, you are pleasure being so you easily yielded to the proposition that pain is an enemy. When you are in pain you feel unfortunate or guilty and believe that there is something wrong with you or somebody is out there to hurt you. Such a teaching is not in harmony with nature and when all through life you have lived by it, your life will be devoid of the peace you crave to experience.

What is natural is to see pain as an ally and a catalyst for your highest good. You and all people want to have a sense of achievement and that requires that you be provided with pain or obstacles to embrace and break through.

You are welcome to Life. You have embarked upon the eternal journey of self-determination and conscious self-actualization that we call Life. By whatever means you came here, you have already boarded the Life Ship and there is no turning back. You better learn how it works and begin to enjoy it to the full.

You were chosen to come into this world and, in turn, you chose to come. In other words, you conspired with Life to be here at this time and in the manner that you came. The fact that you were chosen means you were ripe for this life journey. Also, you must have believed in yourself to choose to come. There was no compulsion. You agreed with the process of life.

If you were not to be here, where would you be and what would that life be like? The Creator feels good about every space of His/Her creation. Wherever you find yourself, you are abiding in the space He/She created. Not all souls have this opportunity to be chosen and not all are ripe to nominate themselves. You must be special and must have believed in yourself to choose this life. Where you are and what is happening is exactly what you signed up for.

If you are temporarily confused, that is okay. Your spiritual creation is like the birthing of the sun from the darkness. You may be in the dawn of your life. Others are in their midmorning, noonday, or twilight. This world is your home; you are not just passing through. Unpack your baggage, get to work, and begin to participate consciously in it and enjoy it.

Life is really a game of Pain and Pleasure that evokes self-definition and conscious self-actualization. To understand what I mean, let's liken the Intelligent Force of the Universe, called God, to the sun and liken you to a ray of light emanating from the sun. Your Being contains the spectrum of Infinite Colors (potentialities). It is one thing to know you have these attributes and another to be conscious of them. You want to see, feel, taste, hear, and experience each color and define through them the virtues that you are.

Take a look at the infinite colors that exist within light, each representing a virtue of the soul. That is what you want to define and be conscious of, and it is an infinite task. By living, you have chosen to actualize the colors, virtues and attributes inherent within you as you. That is what I mean by self-definition and conscious self-actualization.

To fulfill this wondrous goal, you caused the waters of your personal Earth to rise and form clouds. These clouds are resistances to your free expression, the necessary restrictions or pains you need. And when you pass through the clouds like a ray of light, you break into the spectrum of rainbow colors (that represent your potentialities). You thus become self-defined and your inherent virtues become actualized.

So, you see, you need the clouds, the resistance, and the pain to break out and reveal the spectrum of your divine potentialities or virtues. Look at Life. It is a game of Pain and Pleasure. Those who understand this are never disturbed, anxious, or overwhelmed by either of these. And this is the foundation of true wisdom, peace, and enlightenment.

Nature did not intend life to be smooth. It presents you with mountains and valley. No river goes to the ocean in a straight path; it meets with obstacles and works its way through meandering paths. The seeming obstacles become the opportunity for us to build magnificent spectacles on mountain tops and river paths. A straight road over long distances may cause drivers to sleep and that will result in fatal accidents; so, roads must have curves.

Life is about pain but pain is not about you. Pain is about the revelation and expansion of your God magnificence. When God is likened to the sun, you as its ray are the carrier of its magnificence and you are here to express it.

When your big head passed through the narrow birth canal, it was painful to you and to your mother; it was the necessary process that gave birth to you and joy to your mother. Going to school was painful; its result is a sense of achievement that everyone craves. Neither Jesus, the Buddha, nor Krishna escaped pain.

What is natural is for your use. The force of gravity is natural; you cannot destroy it; you just have to find how to use it. It prevents you from jumping high; it virtually keeps you down. Yet, without the force of gravity you cannot walk or play games. You use the force of gravity for games like soccer and basketball, and by studying gravity you even use it for flying. What an immense benefit the force of gravity is! Similarly, pain is the necessary resistance needed for you to play the game of life; play on. It is silly to lament over the force of gravity and equally silly to lament over pain. Just as no one has worried about the force of gravity, you must not worry about pain. Rather embrace it and take it in stride.

Claiming Your Life

Emotions are energies in motion. Pain generates negative emotions. Every negative emotion has a positive intention. When you find that intention, it supports your growth. Dialogue with your negative emotions until they reveal their positive intentions.

It is not necessary to make a litany of your pains. Everyone by age eighteen has suffered shame, guilt, regret, fear, anger and boastful pride; has been ill, has lost something precious; been abused, betrayed, rejected or denied what is his/her right. The list is endless. And, so what? Anyone who laments about any of these pains is just repeating his or her litany of woes. In spite of them, many have made it to greatness; while others have sunk into oblivion. Which of these two courses was chosen is simply the result of a decision that was made. The key word here is DECISION.

Those who are living a life of power are those who decided to use all their pain as tools and catalysts for growth. Such people faced their pain, captured the learning from pain, and moved on to growth.

Many others decided to nurse their pain. They found something to blame and hung on to it. They decided to use their pain to solicit existing and non-existing sympathies. Some may sympathize for a little while; however, they have their own survival needs to attend to and are busy attending to them rather than sympathizing with another.

In any case, even if the whole world sympathizes with you, it is you who suffers and may continue to suffer. Those sufferers are always finding or creating excuses for remaining small and for falling into other series of pain. By the laws of life, you attract what you are; and when your psyche is filled with pain you attract more of it. This means that those who think, feel, or believe that life is difficult will continue to experience difficulties. For them, therefore, life is cruel. When that is your belief, you attract more of the same.

What happens to you in life is not important. It is what you make out of life learning opportunities that matters. Success stories are tales of triumphs over trials; victories over victimization. Make it your determination to create success stories out of your trials.

Pain and Pleasure

If you run from pain throughout your life, that is a problem in itself. This attitude entangles you in more pain. You are always looking for whoever will promise to take you away from pain and you rush to any such promises. The pain you run away from you run into because your mind is focused on what you run away from and will attract more of it. The pain you embrace you master or transform into good. You do not need to suffer pain. To suffer pain is to allow your life to be run, motivated, or dictated to by pain. When you face up to pain you handle it and the power of your genius is increased and made nobler to handle future pains. When you are mature enough to handle pain you become a solution center to pain. In such a state, pain no longer visits you. The light does not admit darkness; similarly, the solution center you become through the mastery of past pains dissolves any future pain before it surfaces.

Pain has a divine duty; to break out the glory of your soul. Pain came for you to identify your capabilities and celebrate your achievements. When the pain is not embraced, you are unconscious of your achievement and deny yourself the nourishment of your achievement. When you recall and celebrate your achievements, they nourish you and empower you for yet greater achievements. Celebrate your achievements and your psyche will be charged with energy that will draw the right people to you and provide you with the right ideas for greater achievements. You will not, however, be able to fully embrace your achievements until you embrace the difficulties, resistances, or pain you broke through.

Pain and pleasure are inseparable twins. You cannot have just one side of the coin. Your embrace of pain makes it a supporting energy for your growth and advancement. Success is the breaking through of barriers. For example, going to school is the breaking through of a knowledge barrier. Think of the joy you feel as a result of having had a successful education. So, I say pain is the reason you are here living your life; but pain is not about you; it is about the activation and articulation of your potentialities.

When you see pain as an ally instead of an enemy, pain loses its ability to hurt you. What you need is a change of attitude about pain. You must outgrow the attitude of "it must not happen to me." Step into the attitude of "every condition I go through will reveal greater good in my life." Welcome pains and afflictions with the positive expectancy of the greater glory that will emanate from them. If you are willing to face pain, it cannot hurt.

You are not some weakling dumped on earth. You are a god, here to define itself and enjoy its attributes. You are not here to chicken out or pass through life unscathed. Pain hurts only when you never deal with it. You are here to handle life. Whatever you can face, you can handle. Face pain and you will always handle it. To the degree that you embrace both pain and pleasure and use them for your highest good, you are real.

Pain believes in you and considers you a god who needed whatever learning it has in store for you. When pain is not handled, it is filed in your unconscious mind until you are ready for it. While residing in the unconscious mind, it attracts its like unto you. It may thus cause you to be triggered to overreact or cloud your vision and blur your understanding.

Free yourself from the selfishness of "why me" and embrace the pain. Over time, you will gain mastery over your pain and then you do not need to suffer it, because you have developed the strength of spirit to make a "light meal" of every pain.

Pain Is Not Punishment

Over the years, you have been deeply programmed to believe that pain is wrong, that it is an evil or punishment from Life for the wrongs you have done, and that good times are blessings from Life for the good you have done. With this notion, mankind created an imaginary monster, called the devil, who is responsible for the pain they experience. Pain is, therefore, seen as yielding to this "devil" and many theologies have it that with the increase of your errors, you will one day have to live with this devil in eternal pain. You, therefore, work to resist pain at all costs; and what you resist, you give attention to and energize it to persist. The devil picture produces fear that is a shade of pain; so in running away from pain, mankind has created a monster for pain.

Whenever one mentions "karma" in Eastern theology it carries the connotation of punishment. When one is in pain, therefore, he/she looks for sins committed to warrant the pain or engages in witch hunting. In so doing, past errors are brought into focus. By the law of the mind, what is focused on is increased; so these people end up worsening their plight. We seem to live in a pain-trapped world. With such a teaching as the foundation of all humanity, you can understand why the peace we crave deep within is not realized; and with such a teaching, it will not ever be realized.

You are not punished for your past or for the errors of the moment. It is not punishment; it is an opportunity to activate and shine forth an attribute of God. No one punishes or rewards. The good you experience is a platform for higher good. If you become content with the good happening in your life, you will be stagnant and will cease to bring forth your higher goodness. Your past errors teach you; they do not punish you. When you embrace the pain quickly, you will find the learning and move into joy.

Giving Up

There is no victory crown in giving up. Everyone knows how to do that. Success stories are made up of the material and substance of challenges, pains, mistakes, and problems. Your attitude should be, "I turn every challenge into a success story!"

Invitation to Wholeness

I invite you to claim your life. Life is not ruled by sympathy or "pity compassion." Life holds the passion to wake you up to your greatness.

Present pains grow on previous ones. If you clear all previous pains, you will have very little in your psyche to attract their like to yourself. Joy grows on previous joys. The more joy you have, the more joy you attract to yourself.

Pain dissolves when you analyze it with a determination to look at its truth. The root causes of most pains are in the ages of conception to eighteen. The pains experienced in these ages, due to the nature of youth, can be exaggerated.

To illustrate, return in your mind to age three and take a look at how tall you saw your father, uncle, or neighbor. Now see the same person through your adult eyes and see how he or she looks smaller or less imposing. Similarly, your mental pictures of shame, betrayal, or abandonment as a child or youth may be grossly exaggerated. In any case, most of the harm done to you was not intended to cause you pain. The malefactors were also pain-trapped; and since pain is all they knew, that is all they could give you. You are, however, entitled to the real you and not to their evil actions or inactions. Life is truly and fully good; so if the pain really happened, it carried life's learning for growth into goodness, resilience of spirit, and greater joy.

For you to see the power of this principle, I will entreat you to do this:

Please close your eyes and probe into yourself several times, asking, "In thinking that life's pains are about me, what could my life be like?"

Come out with all the answers you can. Then probe once more, asking yourself, "In realizing that life's pains are not about me and that they are about the activation and expansion of my inner potentialities, what could my life be like?" Again, come out with several answers and you will feel a shift in consciousness. You will not fail to notice the release and empowerment and that tells you what miracles await you with the practice of these principles.

You Are the Potential

You are a field of infinite potentialities. You do not know what you are or have until you meet the challenge or better still challenge yourself to a great task.

Self Analysis for Freedom from Pain

Realizing that life is about pain and that pain is about your highest good ennobles you to face up to pain with positive expectancy of the good to happen. It thus frees your focus from the pain to its possible good. What you focus on is what you attract and experience.

The person who knows this simple truth is always joyous even in the heat of pain. He or she welcomes pain as a friend and is focused on the certain joy that is emerging. Each pain is not just a challenge; it is an opportunity for a dawning glory.

1. Now I want you to list 50 pains you have experienced.

2. For each of them, list all the joys and learning that emerged.

3. Recall the pain with a determination to find its joy or learning.

Once accomplished, never talk about the pain. Talk about the wondrous joy or learning. For example, when we see the rainbow, we ignore the clouds and speak only of the glorious colors spread across them.

To know why you are what you are is the first step toward recovery from pain and movement to personal growth. Do this recovery process by asking yourself a series of questions several times and then face up to the answers without rationalizing or excusing yourself. For example, you may exercise all of the five regions of your life with the *commands:*

1. Psychologically (emotionally and mentally), why am I what I am today?

2. Spiritually, why am I what I am today?

3. Physically, why am I what I am today?

4. Financially, why am I what I am?

5. Socially, why am I what I am?

Further probes could be these questions: "Truthfully, could something I have experienced been better, or could I have done better?" Write the responses as they reveal themselves.

In living with the old paradigm that life's pains are about you, you live in fear; you are suspicious, angry and tired; you feel unfortunate and live in the "why me" syndrome; you are always looking for someone or something to blame; you feel small and insignificant. You may add others to the list and truly this is not the world you want to live in.

In stepping to the natural principle that life's pains are about the activation of your inner potentialities, you feel empowered; you are filled with passionate adventure; you are eager to know more and celebrate life; you are unafraid and able to face even death with joy; you feel omnipotent and wise. You may add more to this list and truly that is the world you do want to live in. You can create it by practicing this principle.

Lessons on the Principle of Pain

1. Pain is natural so don't make an issue out of it.

2. Present pains grow on previous ones. If you clear all previous pains, you will have very little in your psyche to attract their like to yourself.

3. The pain you run away from, you run into. The pains you confront will surrender their learning for your growth.

4. Use pain for your growth by determining each pain's positive outcome.

Benefits of Principle One

1. When you consider pain as natural, you are not disturbed by its presence and that makes it ineffective on you.
2. You release all past painful memories.
3. You are filled with great courage and enthusiasm when faced with a problem.
4. Nothing overwhelms you.
5. You are in dominion over life and truly happy.

PRINCIPLE 2

The Principle of Wellbeing

Release Yourself from the Need for Apology and Gratitude. No one owes you an apology for harm done you or gratitude for the good you did to them.

No one goes through life without being hurt by another. Generally, you are taught that it is natural to expect those who have hurt you to come clean by accepting their fault, apologizing, and seeking your forgiveness. You will then have the prerogative to offer them forgiveness or not to do so. You, therefore, carry the burden of the hurts done to you. When you scan your mind, you will find many people who must seek your forgiveness. You will also find those you expect to need you some day in the future. The only reason you expect them to need you is that you expect them to atone in some way for some harm done to you. Even if you are ready to forgive, the truth is that it may take very long time for many to realize their errors and seek forgiveness.

These expectations keep you in the prison of vengeance. How do you feel when you think of people who have done you wrong and have not bothered to apologize? The memory of harm done to you gives you bad feelings and generates painful thoughts in you. These bad feelings and thoughts alone are responsible for many physical and emotional ills you may suffer. The need for apology keeps you a prisoner to the pain caused you or you believed or imagined had been caused you. It is an unnecessary suffering.

The Need for Apology

There is a subtle yet powerful force that keeps you prisoner to the hurts you believe have been done to you. It is that you are taught to expect apology as a prerequisite for forgiveness. As a child, when you did something wrong you were routinely required to apologize to regain your parents' favor. Over time, you concluded that those who offend you must apologize to regain your favor. These unnatural conclusions make you wait for an apology that most of the time never comes or delays in coming; and while waiting you are in the prison of pain.

Unsuspecting, you and the world have yielded to this teaching or suggestion that you need an apology. This is an unnatural and unworkable principle to live by. It succeeds in keeping you a prisoner to pain.

The truth is that *"No one owes you apology for any harm done to you."* Everybody's action or inaction that caused you hurt stemmed from limited knowledge and experience; and that has a long history. Their perceived wrong attitudes were not pre-designed to cause you hurt.

A person's action or inaction stems from who their parents are, where they were conceived, their upbringing and early environment, the schools they attended, the religious body or philosophy they grew up with, the friends they grew up with; and the list goes on. You cannot do yourself the injustice of carrying the responsibility of people's errors. People will continue to do wrong; it is you who must design strategies and attitudes for handling wrongdoings

You cannot stop people from doing painful things, but it is up to you to decide what you want to feel about what people do. Almost all of the harm done to you was unintentional. This natural realization will change your attitude toward those you consider to have hurt you. Think of the number of times you have hurt someone even though you did not intend to.

Most things you considered hurt or harm done to you stemmed from your own interpretations and expectations. The bad feelings you have from people's actions or inactions were generated in you by you. You cannot, therefore, blame anyone for the bad feelings that reduce your power. You have the power to handle whatever is inside you, and certainly you can change the feelings you have by changing your expectations and interpretations.

There are millions of interpretations to an event. Choose interpretations that honor you and bring you joy. A victim of rape transcended her pain when she chose to think of the rapist as a child of God. Most rapists are mentally imbalanced, needing treatment. A person does not lose his God identity just because he is ill. The woman relived the experience, looking into the eyes of the rapist and saying to herself, "He is a child of God."

You cannot live without interpretation and expectations. You must, however, be responsible for the feelings they bring you. When you take responsibility for the feelings your expectations and interpretation bring to you, you will be in charge of your response to life and you will have inner peace.

There are others who live with their pain, feeling and believing that life owes them an apology for the hurts they have experienced. They live waiting to be compensated by life for what has been destroyed in their life experiences. What in life is to compensate you – the air, the sky, the earth or what? Life is not conscious of any harm you have experienced. You are on your own authentic journey, using all that life has provided for your highest good. The scripture said, *"All things work for the good of those who trust in God."* All things include good and bad ones. You are to use all for your authentic good.

All people are doing the best they know based on their limited knowledge, experience, and human weakness. What you choose to feel about other people's actions or inactions is your choice. A thief steals due to his human weakness of fear that there is "not enough to go around." It hurts when you are robbed but when you meet the hurt feeling with your God attitude, it dissolves.

Two people each go through a discomfiting event. One comes out of it emotionally battered while the other person comes out of it unscratched. The one who felt very injured is injured by her own expectations and interpretations, which come from her past. Good or bad are not in events; they are in the minds of people.

Making it worse, you carry the guilt for harm you have done to others through your lack of knowledge. Others trap you by making you feel responsible for their bad feelings. You do not owe anyone for his or her bad feelings. Do not succumb to emotional blackmail. If you realize an error that has caused someone harm, you have increased your degree of enlightenment. You owe it to yourself to apologize to the person; it is the act of giving firm rooting to the new knowledge that made you realize the mistake. A mistake realized is knowledge gained. By ignoring the need to apologize, you corrupt the seed of the new knowledge and may not be able to grow it into richer experience.

No one owes you apology for any harm done to you; people owe it to themselves to apologize when they realize their mistakes.

In the same way that it takes some people a long time to see where they went wrong when working with a mathematics equation, it may take people who have hurt you a long time to realize they have caused you pain. Holding on to the pain is like putting your hand in fire or drinking poison and expecting those who have hurt you to suffer.

As a child, functioning from your limited knowledge and experience, you did many wrong things. Today, you forgive those past errors. You do not ask your past actions or inactions to come and apologize. Similarly, though in adult bodies, others are in their infantile and childhood stages in life and may act from their limited knowledge and experience. Choose to forgive them as you did to your own past wrong doings.

There are also people who for fear of hurting someone live a life of cautious isolation. Eventually, they cause harm to many and are overwhelmed when they find out that they have hurt someone. It is impossible to live a life without hurting anyone. People are entitled to their own expectations and interpretations. Your innocent, well-intentioned action or inaction may be interpreted through the eyes of these people's own pain, leading them to conclude that you have hurt them; it is normal for such to happen. Your cautious attitude of not wanting to hurt anyone will blind you to subtle details in your actions and inactions that are erroneous and you may unconsciously cause genuine harm to many. A useful way is to live with genuine intention for the good of all and then to lose yourself in action, trusting the best possible outcome. When you live this way, you will be in a state of mind to own up to error and to correct it immediately. This is life. Be part of its wonderful drama.

Apologize Graciously

The drive for heroism makes many people blind themselves to the wrongs they commit. They will go to any extent to rationalize and justify themselves even when the facts stare them in the face. Waiting for apology from such people is a waste of time and you remain in prison.

It is noble to recognize your errors and apologize readily and graciously when you realize you are wrong. Many consider being wrong as shameful so they resist owning up to it. To be wrong is normal and natural.

When you disown the error you disown the learning also and that shuts your door to the fountain of knowledge and wisdom. You thus deny yourself the good of the universe.

To own up to error is an admission of wrongdoing. When as a child you did something wrong, you were punished and you lost favor. You felt blacklisted and placed in the bad books of somebody. You felt the whole world was screaming at you and labeling you a wrongdoer. Who would want that to happen? Something inside you may accept that you did wrong but rejects the label of a wrongdoer. Ever since you felt labeled in that way, you resist owning up to errors and fight to escape anything that has to do with your being a wrongdoer. So you are constantly running away from errors you committed.

By running away from your errors your mind is focused on them and, in accordance with the law of the mind, you attract what you focus on; thus, you go through repeated mistakes. What a waste!

To apologize for wrongdoing is a sign of growth and maturity, and nature is about growth. Apologizing is an admission that you are willing to learn, that you have learned and are ready to be more. By the admission of your errors, you are simply saying that you are wiser today than you have ever been.

Admitting you made an error does not throw you into jail; it is the denial of error that makes you repeat errors until you end up in jail. And contrary to what you may think, when you admit your error you are respected; the other person feels you are gracious and can be trusted. On the other hand, in the course of denial of error you may pretend in your feelings and actions; however, in your mind you know the truth. With the truth staring you in the face you begin to quarrel and fight with yourself and thus waste valuable mental energy that could be used for progress. There are many who have run away from their errors for so long that these people make the lie their truth and are thus partially or completely numb to their wrongdoings. At the extreme, they become insensitive to all wrong doing.

Everything in life was once a mistake. New inventions of products are simply attempts to correct errors in the precious ones. Even software designed by the computer giants comes with lots of bugs that are constantly being fixed. Error is natural. It adds to the excitement of life. Owning up to error is the only way of lifting yourself above the error. When you refuse to own up to your errors, you remain a constant wrongdoer in your mind. Your errors do not make you less. It is noble to accept them and to use the magic statement, "I am sorry." That statement heals the wounds of the offended, lifts your vision to a wealth of greater possibilities, and wins you allies for growth.

The Need for Gratitude

Not only do you carry the burden of harms done to you, you also carry the burden of gratitude denied to you. When people do not show the gratitude you believe they should show for the good you have done for them, how do you feel and what decisions do you make as a result?

Think of the attitudes you have cultivated as a result of people's failure to express gratitude to you. Most of these attitudes do not reflect your true nature. The need for the gratitude that has been denied you makes you not want to do good for anyone, so you stop yourself from doing and being the good you are. When you stop yourself from doing good, you block the flow of divine goodness through you. The good that flows through you, blesses you and you must not stop it. To stop it is to stop the expression of your greatness. Blocking it is the unnecessary wreaking of vengeance on yourself for the slow growth of another person.

Many people are grateful but only a few know how to show it. Some show it but due to cultural or social differences, they either do not show it the way you are accustomed to or you are not appreciative of their way of showing gratitude. To reclaim yourself consider that if all of the people who should have shown you gratitude had done so, what sort of person would you be? Step into that person now, for it is your true nature.

In any case, when people give you the expected gratitude, you have earned your reward. When the good you did is not compensated by a show of gratitude, you are open to the universe to show you that gratitude; and that increases the magnitude of the blessing.

People owe it to themselves to be grateful for the good you do for them. They will feel good, healed, and complete if they do. You have no business demanding them to show you gratitude. Your business is to do the good you know to do and that's all there is to it. You owe it to yourself to be grateful and to realize where you have failed to do so, then to make amends and offer gratitude.

Breaking the Vessel of Pain

The practice of this principle alone will bring you great freedom and unleash your potentialities. At this point, allow your eyes to close and say, "*No one owes me an apology for any harm done to me.*" Repeat this statement a few times. You can see in your mind's eye all of the people to whom this applies. You can feel the release. Through doing this practice, forgiveness is granted.

No one owes you an apology for harm done you or gratitude for the good you did for them. If God were expecting your apology or gratitude for every next move, imagine the chaos that would happen. Many people are trapped in the spirit of vengeance for too long. To need apology or gratitude is a vengeance drive. The vengeance drive wants people who have hurt you to come to you feeling sorry or begging for your forgiveness; then you will have the prerogative to give forgiveness to them or deny it to them. The vengeance drive also wants people you have helped and who have not shown gratitude to be in need someday and to come to you for help so you will have a chance to obtain the gratitude you are waiting for. These opportunities may take a long time in coming; meanwhile, you are in the prison of stored pain.

Similarly, you do not owe anyone an apology for the harm you may have done or gratitude for the good done to you. You owe it to yourself to outgrow human weaknesses that cause confusion and harm to others. You owe it to yourself to be appreciative of the good that comes to you. The moment you recognize the harm you have done to someone and make amends is a moment of learning and growth. What you are grateful for and appreciate increases and crystallizes for you. The gratitude you show to people opens you to more goodness.

Have God-attitudes or philosophies for living. One I use for myself is: "Let my heart be broken by the things that break the heart of God."

Recovering Lost Mental Energy

Every move starts with a thought. We are moved by conscious thoughts or preprogrammed reflex thoughts.

In conscious thought, you think then act that thought. In reflex thought, you instinctively move away as if from a hot iron.

The greater part of your life is managed by preprogrammed reflex thoughts. For example, 90% of the entire functioning of your body is through preprogrammed reflex thought; the pumping of blood by the heart, the purification system of the kidneys, the seeing of color by the eyes, etc., are all regulated by preprogrammed reflex thought.

The force of preprogrammed reflex thought is so strong that it pushes its way into areas where conscious inputs are necessary. Preprogrammed reflex thought is intelligent unconscious activity. If it is allowed to take over the thinking processes of the conscious mind, the individual lives a life of unconsciousness. His or her actions are involuntary responses to external stimuli and are controlled by the environment, much in the way that an unconscious organism functions.

Little though your conscious inputs might be, they are responsible for how the large energy field of preprogrammed reflex thought serves your life.

By needing apology from people who have hurt you and gratitude from those for whom you have done good, you reduce your mental field to a quarreling playground, and finally you lose possession of it. Quarreling thoughts cause stress and stress-related diseases; they waste your mental and emotional energies and they drain you.

Conscious Recovery

Calculate how much conscious thought you possess and you will be inspired to increase it. Here is a simple probe to help you with this calculation.

How much of your mental time do you spend in quarreling? Quarreling thoughts include all the people you are arguing with and complaining about in your mind.

From the responses to the above probe, you will realize you have been and are wasting vast stocks of mental energy that may be used for something more creative or valuable.

Other probes are:

How much of your internal conversations are you in charge of?

How much of your thoughts are solution-oriented or just wandering thoughts?

A conscious input into your thought processes will demand that the thoughts produce conclusive results or solutions. When your thoughts are so directed, you will soon realize that solutions come to you fast and easy and that you have time to create future good. When the mind gets you into wandering quarrels, pause and ask yourself, "What solution is there to this problem or what good do I want to experience out of this?" Soon your mind will begin to birth solutions. It will begin to hear your voice and obey your will. When it cannot hear your voice, you cannot exercise your will over the external.

Observe your thoughts. You are either in unnecessary mental quarrels and arguments or in solution and creative thoughts. Mental arguments and quarrels can result in accidents and disease. Many times when you have bitten your tongue you were involved in mental arguments and quarrels.

Freedom from the Trap of the Need for Apology and Gratitude

1. Allow your eyes to close and make this statement several times. "No one owes me an apology for any wrong done to me. Everyone did what they knew based on their limited knowledge and experience." You may substitute this statement with any that inspired you when you read through this principle.

2. As you make the statement, listen to your life and notice what past events this is addressing.

3. When you find an event that this statement is addressing, locate yourself at the beginning of that event. To be sure you are in that event, notice what you are seeing, hearing, tasting, smelling, and feeling. While in that event, make the statement several times. Look into the faces of the person or persons involved and make the statement.

4. Do steps one to three several times, allowing the process to address other cuds or to stimulate abilities.

5. Repeat steps one to three, this time with the statement, "No one owes me gratitude for the good I have ever done. I was not forced to do that good. It is my true nature to do that good and to continue to do it."

Lessons on the Principle of Apology and Gratitude

1. You do not owe anyone an apology. You owe it to yourself to recognize your errors and make amends.

2. You do not owe anyone gratitude. You owe it to yourself to show gratitude. What you are grateful for and appreciate increases and crystallizes for you.

3. Your pains are mostly caused by your expectations and interpretations of events.

4. Expecting gratitude stops you from expressing the loveliness and beauty you are and this robs you from the gift you are to yourself.

Benefits of Principle Two

1. You are free from all injuries you believed people caused you. Thus you can love your past and embrace the moment.

2. You are free from the prison of guilt.

3. You do not see errors to forgive so you are always clean in mind and feeling.

PRINCIPLE 3
The Principle of Community Building

Release yourself from the need to be understood.

Besides food, the most demanding need of everyone is the desire to be understood. When you are understood you feel heard, loved, accepted, and honored. To be understood makes you feel that you are receiving the needed attention and care. As a child, you were taught to feel that it is the right thing to be understood or need attention. Parents feel happy when their children need them so children are encouraged to do so.

This unnatural demand is the cause for the greater part of your woes in this world.

Nature's Principle of Understanding

Nature or God, or whatever you choose to call it, did not create you to be understood; you are not meant to be understood and such an expectation keeps you in bondage. Nature did not create you to be readable. If you were, you would lose the magic and the mystery, and that would end the exploration and adventure of life. For example, if you can predict your every move and the every move of others, you will soon be bored with yourself and with life. Nature created you a complex and mysterious being, too mysterious to be understood.

As children, you needed the attention that understanding brings. The natural way of growth is to successfully release that need. The need to be understood is an indication of a person who has not grown.

People can understand you based on their own history but such understanding can never be comprehensive. To understand someone is to "stand under" the person's history and this is not possible to do with someone else's history. It requires that you understand where the person was conceived, where he grew up, the schools he attended, the religion he belonged to, the friends he had, and the problems he has been through. The list is endless and it is an impossible riddle to solve. Man is a complex summation of histories.

The truth is that you do not know and understand yourself fully, how can you expect that someone else will understand you? There may have been times you sought to explain yourself regarding an issue and you could not find the words to do so. Then the other person expressed what you were trying to say and you agreed that the other person had explained your thoughts better. This is an indication that you do not know or understand yourself completely; in fact, even if you do understand yourself in a specific instance, you do not always have the exact words or language to verbalize that understanding perfectly. So even if someone understands you, how can you expect that they will find the appropriate words to explain their understanding? You are too mysterious and complex to understand yourself completely. This mystery and complexity speaks of the beauty, magic, and wonderment of your life. For example, after twenty years of marriage, a spouse realizes that he suddenly does not understand his partner. This should not come as a surprise because in each moment we are unfolding something more of ourselves.

Five people returned from the safari where they had had a great time. Asked how they enjoyed it, one spoke about the smell of the forest grounds and the smell of the flowers; another spoke about the beautiful colors of the flowers, birds, and animals; another spoke about the melodious sounds of the birds and cooing sounds of the forest animals; yet another spoke about the exotic taste of the rare fruits; and the last spoke about the ambience of the forest atmosphere.

These people, like everyone else, were operating from their senses of smell, sight, sound, taste, and feel respectively. Most people operate largely from one or two senses only. Few, however, are full multi-sensory. Thus a woman who is dominant in hearing may appreciate the latest car her husband bought for her but will still feel unloved until she hears him say, "I love you." Each person is a complex energy field that processes information in complex ways. And most people have only one or two dominant sense or two for processing data; the rest of their senses are minor. The roles of all of these senses change with time and with the issues at hand. It is too complex to analyze and appreciate fully; participate in the magic of just being able to communicate intelligibly with another person.

To be happy and free, release yourself from the need to be understood. You are too complex to be understood. You are a mystery and a wonderment of God that is constantly unfolding. You do not know exactly what you are going to do or be in the next moment. You surprise yourself each moment. God lost the mold He used to create you so there is no one else like you. There can neither be anyone to be compared to you; nor can you be understood by or through another person's standards. You are a mystery to be explored, a gift that is being unwrapped. You are simply unique in every way. Embrace the mystery that you are and pray to understand you. No one owes you understanding and no one is to be blamed for not understanding you. No one who does not know your complete past can understand you. All people interpret you according to their limited knowledge and experience and that is all right. It is your duty to discover you and explain you. Catch a new you in each moment. The sun has no need to be understood. It simply shines and we interpret it by using it in various forms of technology. It is unrealistic to expect to be understood.

The Measure of Understanding

Give thanks if someone captures a glimpse of you in their understanding and be grateful if you understand something of someone for a moment. What you understand in a moment about someone is a gift of God to you. Give thanks for that gift but do not use it as a measure to understand that person in the future because all people are changing moment by moment. A person is made up of forty-six chromosomes, which carry the genes of many generations. The life pattern of a generation may surface at any time in a person's life and there is no means of predicting that.

The mystery of life is to make yourself understood if even for a moment. For this to happen, you must be able to express yourself without the expectation that the other person will understand you. The other person must also be free from his past and its prejudices in order to be available to understand you. It is a divine gift to make yourself be understood. In making your divine complexity be understood, you bring yourself the gift of knowing yourself. However, a need to be understood causes strain, which blocks your psychic pathways and thus blocks your wisdom, and you need wisdom to explain the complex you. The need to be understood, therefore, makes you unavailable to be understood. Think of the pretenses you use in an attempt to be understood. The need to be understood advertises something that is unlike you and this makes it difficult for you to be understood. For example, when you are preoccupied with what you want to say in a conversation while the other person is still speaking, you may be pretending to listen but you do not hear all that is said. When you eventually get the chance to speak, you may be out of sync with what the other person was saying. What you then say may cause the other person to wonder where you are coming from. This creates confusion. Being preoccupied made you unavailable to hear or be heard. Similarly, needing to be understood makes you unavailable to understand or be understood. To understand and be understood, make yourself available by releasing yourself from the need to be understood.

RELEASE YOURSELF FROM THE NEED TO BE UNDERSTOOD. THEN YOU WILL BE AVAILABLE TO UNDERSTAND AND BE UNDERSTOOD.

The Need to Be Pleased

Similarly, release yourself from the need to be pleased. No one can please you. When you are pleased, it happens because you accepted the offer of someone's best. It is your acceptance that pleased you. All people are on their authentic journey doing the best they know. When you are displeased, it speaks of the mystery that you are. It is your call to find out from yourself the frequency you need to vibrate from in order to relate to the other person. You are a field of infinite frequencies. For every situation, there is a frequency in you that enables you to relate to that situation. You may observe, for example, that when you are upset you do not find pleasure even in the most joyful events. In that state, you have shifted your frequency. Be in the state of "I am tuning myself to be pleased," and you will.

RELEASE YOURSELF FROM THE NEED TO BE PLEASED.

Reclaiming Your Love Energy

The love you feel is a gift from God. Celebrate it! Often you destroy this gift by expecting the love you give to be reciprocated. The love you feel heals and rejuvenates you. The cells of your body rejoice when you wash them in the energy of love. Do it. Loving someone does not require the person to reciprocate. To expect the other person to do so is to turn the love energy into curse energy. You feel bitter when the love you are expecting to be reciprocated is not forthcoming. That bitterness wounds the cells of your body, hurts your feelings, and blurs your thinking.

Love is the elixir of life that heals and rejuvenates you. When someone or something activates it, you have been blessed through that person, condition, or thing. You must give yourself the space and time to celebrate it.

The love you have for someone is your personal possession. Even if the person you love is not conscious of your love, you have found your secret elixir and the love you feel is important to you. Love does not necessarily result in a relationship. You may nurse love for billions of souls and that enlarges and enriches you. You may be divorced but you must not lose the love that once existed in your relationship. That is your possession. The love energy you activate in you varies from person to person in color and force and each expression of love enriches you in a special and unique way.

Be available to enjoy the love you give away. "The love you give away you keep." The love you give away is the only love you need. That love is unique in nature and vibration and it is impossible for anyone to match it or reciprocate it. Be still and enjoy the magic you feel in love, for its energy is as unique as yourself.

When you release the person you love to be himself or herself; then there is no pretense. And if the person gives his or her attention to another, so be it. Because you love that person you feel good that what you love is in great joy. You simply enjoy the joy of the one you love.

Love freely and do not put measurements to it. Feel the goodness of the love you feel and let it honor you. You wanted to be sure that you are loved for you to love. In so doing, you stopped yourself from loving. You have practiced stopping yourself from loving for so long that you need to heal. Let your love flow out freely; let it touch all men, beasts, animals, trees, and the elements. Let your love swell to touch the center of the universe.

RELEASE YOURSELF FROM THE NEED TO EXPERIENCE RECIPROCATION OF YOUR LOVE.

What Motivates You

Check the motivation for your love. You are motivated either by a sense of self-acceptance or by a need to be accepted because you fear rejection. You are motivated either by love or by anger and fear. You are motivated either by the drive to give out love or to receive love. You are motivated either by a vision of possibilities or by a fear of lack. What is motivating you is what you eventually experience.

When you release yourself from the need to be understood, you accept yourself; you walk into a crowd confidently, knowing that it is okay even if you are not understood. You love yourself and this enables you to be conscious of the love that surrounds you as well as the love you give out. The release from the need to be understood frees you from the need to defend yourself. Your self image is universal and is ever changing.

A Meaning of Rejection

Fear is one of the greatest diseases of mankind, and one of the greatest fears of all time is the fear of rejection. Rejection makes you feel unwanted, unaccepted, not belonging to, defeated and shamed.

The application of this principle gives you instant dominion over rejection. It provides you with a new meaning of it. Rejection for the most part is advertisement of the other person's ignorance, imploring you to prepare the right "medication" for it. What people cannot understand they laugh at or scorn, using their laughter as a cover up for their ignorance. In fact, they are demonstrating their own ignorance and inferiority. Many people may reject you for what they reject in themselves. Check it out; what people do not like in themselves is what they see and reject in others, so you are not the target. For fear of rejection, you may stop yourself from being or doing the good you are capable of or you may stop sharing the truth you believe in. Rejection by others may actually be evidence that your wisdom, experience, or expertise is superior to theirs. It is also the confirmation of the mystery and magic that you are. Therefore, do not stop yourself from being what you are or doing what you know is best.

In doing your best you may sometimes get things wrong and that is also okay, because in realizing the error you become wiser than you have ever been before and that is wonderful. Rejection cannot stop you. Listen to the cry for help in rejection and be willing to design new ways of providing solutions. A healthy person would not reject you when you are wrong but instead would support you in learning. If people reject you when you are wrong about something, they are rejecting what is wrong in themselves that they cannot live with. A person who tells lies is suspicious of the stories of other people and considers them as possible lies. The rejection of your story is the rejection by that person of his own lying attitude.

The Practice of Understanding

Again, when you release yourself from the need to be understood, forgiveness automatically results. To release yourself, return in your mind to the past; revisit all events in which you were misunderstood or felt so. In each event simply say with inner knowing, "I release myself from the need to be understood. Freed from the need to be understood, what is the taste, sound, smell, feel, and vision of that event?" Make this your fifteen-minute morning meditation. Your past will be forgiven, releasing your locked up spiritual energy previously trapped in pain.

Dreamers and Their Calling

Dreamers are those who are open to the Universal Intelligence that is pouring itself out into manifestation. They capture universal ideas that grow in them into realities. To dream is to have clear and vivid mental and emotional picture of a possible reality. It is a clear knowing of what is possible yet not manifest. The dream does not belong to the dreamer; it belongs to God, the Universal Intelligence, and as such is always bigger than the dreamer.

Sadly, many people lose touch with their magnificence because they abandoned their dreams for fear of not being understood. The dream is in the mind of the dreamer and no one sees the dream. Therefore, it is normal if you are not understood. If your dream makes you lose friends and the understanding of men; if it looks enormous and impossible of achievement; if its enormity sometimes frightens you, makes your bones shake and quake, then you know for certain that you have a big dream calling you into the expansion of yourself. If it feels frightening, huge or impossible; if it feels dangerous and out of place, then you have a dream and a calling to manifest it. Give it all your internal and external resources. In so doing God is glorified as you.

Dream the impossible, then ask yourself, "Why not?" and move into action, never looking back. The dream calls you to work.

If you see the possibility and no one else sees it, then you have a calling to bring it forward to manifestation and to the awareness of other people. It is impossible for a feather to remain flying or suspended in space. Someone dreamt of flying and today a whole village could fly in an aircraft across oceans. Just twenty years ago, it was impossible to conceive of the cellular phone; today it is a reality and you can talk with your loved ones across the distances.

It is not a calling if what you want to achieve is common knowledge. Feel special and do your dream and do not be anxious about being successful; be faithful, for your success is with Spirit. The success of great dreams cannot be measured by human yardsticks. Success is not about numbers, volume or human patronage. It is about the quality of your spirit. The magnitude of the dream speaks of the magnitude of respect the universe has for you and you cannot deny yourself the opportunity to expand yourself. The bigger the dream is, the bigger the opportunity to enlarge your own soul. Be sure to do it and do it well, with passion and life force. Such dreams are supported by the entire universe. No fulfillment of a dream goes unrewarded.

You must live for something. Let it make a difference that you lived. If need be, die for your dream. It's a transient life; thunder through it. Such are the souls who leave a legacy of wealth in their names to the extent that the mere mentioning of their names brings joy and life to all who utter it and to all who hear it.

When you see the dream of the dreamer, then you are a co-dreamer and in that you have a calling and an equal responsibility as the dreamer to make it happen. The dreamer has only tuned you to the dream in the Universal Intelligence. In the same way that all radios may tune in to a station and receive the same information, you are tuned in. If the first dreamer happens to sleep, you have the role of carrying on. If the first dreamer is active in fulfilling the dream, you are to be his partner in making it happen. Remember that you have an equal responsibility to make the dream happen. Do not be in the shadow of the first dreamer; be the catalyst and if need be run the vehicle.

I am one of such dreamers. I have a dream that many may consider crazy. I believe that I can cause a mass change in the world to produce true world peace in my lifetime. When I look at where the world is today, it seems really impossible and it frightens me to think that I may die without accomplishing this. I have prayed, researched into the human spirit, discovered workable principles like the ones you find in this book, and developed tools to make this dream happen. I have developed a program, known as Growing the Empowered Child, for cleansing children from fear and anger and restoring them to their sense of uniqueness. I intend to make this program available to every home. Everyone who gets a taste of the program agrees that it will heal and change the world for peace. I have co-dreamers who are supporting me in spreading the word, but the progress is too slow for my liking and I spend sleepless nights, fine tuning the programs for mass education. In spite of all of the setbacks, I have no doubt that this planet will see peace in my lifetime and by your reading of this book I know that you are part of the team. I will neither be stopped nor can I stop myself; I would rather do something great and not succeed than do nothing. My clear conviction is that I will succeed.

Dream. Do your dream and remember that it is okay not to be understood.

A Release and Empowerment Program on Understanding

1. Allow your eyes to close and make this statement several times. "*I release myself from the need to be understood. I am a mystery to be discovered.*" You may substitute this statement with any that inspired you when you read through this principle.

2. As you make the statement listen to your life and notice what past events this is addressing.

3. When you find an event this statement is addressing, locate yourself at the beginning of that event. To be sure you are in that event, notice what you are seeing, hearing, tasting, smelling, and feeling. While in that event, make the statement several times. Look into the faces of the person or persons involved and make that statement.

4. Repeat the above three steps several times, allowing them to address other cuds or to stimulate abilities.

5. Open your eyes then make the release statement below several times. You may add to the statement as your spirit directs.

The Release Practice

I return to the past and successfully release all who misunderstood me. And I release myself from all moments of feeling misunderstood.

I release all abuses I experienced, knowing that no one intends evil for me. Everyone acted on their limited knowledge and experience. The abuse is not meant against me. It is the advertisement of people's maturity and their cry for me to do something more.

Lessons on the Principle of Understanding

1. You are a mystery; you cannot be fully understood.

2. You don't understand yourself; so it is not possible for others to understand you.

3. What you understand of a person in a moment is a gift from life; celebrate it but do not use that as a measurement of what they must be in the future.

4. It is okay if you do not understand others; just enjoy them and the magic and mystery of the moment.

5. Needing to be understood makes you unavailable to understand or be understood.

6. You do not need the love of the other person to love him or her. Your love is your rich possession; nurse and celebrate it.

Benefits of Principle Three

1. It restores confidence and the sense of freedom. You move easily into a group and speak your mind or take your action because you are not disturbed by whether the people in the group understand you or not.

2. This practice makes you creative and unafraid to experiment several times, because you are uninfluenced by people's opinions.

3. You are passionately joyful because you participate in the mystery and the magic of the moment and you celebrate the wonderment that everyone is.

4. You are authentic.

PRINCIPLE 4
The Principle of Freedom

Release Yourself from the Need to Control, Rule, and Possess Others.
Claim Your Freedom By Releasing Your Prisoners.

The drive to rule and control others has become an imperative. Everyone wants to dominate or rule over someone else; tribes want to rule over other tribes and nations want to rule over other nations. Everyone is looking for a territory to rule or control. People marry or have children to get someone to rule. Others use all sorts of tricks, such as crying, to manipulate another. Manipulation is a drive to control or rule the other person.

While seeking to rule over people, you resist being ruled over. When you are ruled over in your work place, you then may want to rule over the people in your household. It is your way of freeing yourself from being dominated in the work place or wherever you feel you are dominated.

Created by an omnipotent, omnipresent and omniscience presence and vested with its power, you have a drive for omnipotence and that is natural. This is the drive which is being wrongly applied when you want to rule over others. Ruling over others gives a sense of power but it is a false one. The need to have power over others is the recognition of their power, and in trying to get power over them you lose touch with your omnipotence. Omnipotence means that power extends through all units of life.

Each person comes from the same source that you came from and so is vested with omnipotence. You cannot, therefore, control such an omnipotent and complex being as man is. You may achieve something that looks and feels like control; however, in reality you are imprisoning yourself. You do not dominate by ruling over; you dominate by ruling with. When you dominate others you create a prison, because, for as long as you dominate others, they fight you for their freedom. It is like keeping a cork under water. It is forever seeking an upward thrust. When your hands are tired, the cork resurfaces. The key is to have power with someone. You are in true power when you see the individualized power in each person as extensions of your own power. The desire to rule or control others always creates conflict and confusion. All nations that have ruled over others have eventually fallen and so it will continue to be.

Each human being is a very large spiritual presence and you are too full to contain another magnificent being in yourself. You are a mystery and a magic constantly unfolding and so are all persons you meet. Freedom and the right to be are imperative, and anyone you rule over will fight you for those rights.

The drive to control or rule over others scatters the conscious presence you need in order to celebrate your own magnificence. It also engages your energy in a fight. You will always be thinking of what to do to subjugate the other person. When you release the need to control or rule over people, you become available to enjoy more of you.

Release yourself from the need to control or rule others because such will imprison you.

You are a ruler when you rule yourself and not when you rule other people. In seeking to control or rule others you lose touch with what you must really rule. The only way of ruling that gives comfort is when you rule yourself. Take dominion over your thoughts and feelings and you are a true ruler.

Find power in the mystery of relating with people. Everyone you meet is a packet of mystery. The ability to communicate and receive communication from people is a mystery – enjoy it. Enjoy the wonderment, the pure bliss of being able to speak with another person.

Never attempt to possess another person. It is impossible. If you do not possess your own self; your thoughts and feelings keep racing, one after the other; then how do you hope to possess another? The real being is not the body that walks. Man is more than a walking machine. Man is a spirit being. Man can be compared to the moonbeam, which it is to be enjoyed while it is available. You cannot possess or rule it.

You may keep a man's body in prison but you cannot imprison his mind and feelings; and that is where the person really resides.

You may have a spouse and children. You do not truly possess them. In fact, man is too mysterious to be possessed. Human beings are not meant to be ruled or controlled. They may yield to you for a little while, especially when they are getting a benefit from succumbing. So in effect they are also exploiting you.

He is rich who possesses himself and not he who possesses the earth. Man is a complex system of thoughts feelings and the influence of their histories. You do not possess your own thoughts and feelings; how do you hope to possess someone else?

To possess yourself requires much work, so start possessing yourself instead of attempting to possess another.

You lose power the moment you think of ruling over someone, because such a drive makes you see power outside yourself.

There is an imperative drive for omnipotence and freedom in everyone; it will fight whatever rules it for its freedom. If you want your freedom, first give it to others.

Ruling over another keeps you a prisoner and subjects you to constant fight. The restriction you put on others is the restriction you put on yourself. And when you are preoccupied in developing strategies to keep people under restriction you are not available to enjoy your own life.

Changing People

People want to change people around them but not themselves. The effort to change people to suit your liking is a control drive. This attempt has been and will remain futile. It is too much work and trouble to try to change people. It is easier to change one person, yourself, than to change people around you. Life shifts you into various occupations and you meet people in all walks of life such that it is impossible to change all of them.

A tuning fork will vibrate when its sound is in resonance with another one. For example, if you were vibrating at a frequency number 2 and you are surrounded by people of frequency numbers six, nine, twelve, and fifteen, you will be in harmony with only those of frequency six and twelve. To harmonize with all, you may work on yourself to vibrate at frequency three. It is easier to do that than to work on each tuning fork to change it to your frequency. Similarly, it is easier to change you than to change the 6.5 billion people on the planet.

To change people is to change their history and that is an impossible task. People can learn from their history and use that knowledge to move on.

How to Be Free from the Prison of Control, Rule, and Possessiveness

1. Allow your eyes to close and make this statement several times. "*I release myself from the need to control or dominate another. I am now available to enjoy me.*" You may substitute this statement with any that inspired you when you read through this principle.

2. As you make the statement, listen to your life and notice what past events this is addressing.

3. When you find an event that this statement is addressing, locate yourself at the beginning of that event. To be sure that you are in that event, notice what you are seeing, hearing, tasting, smelling, and feeling. While in that event, make the statement several times. Look into the faces of the person or persons involved and make that statement.

4. Repeat the above three steps several times, allowing them to address other cuds or to stimulate abilities.

5. End your session by allowing your eyes to open.

Lessons on the Principle of Control, Rule and Possessiveness

1. Man is too complex a being to be ruled by another man.

2. You are a ruler when you rule yourself and not when you rule other people.

3. You lose power when you have power over someone else because that person is constantly fighting against you for their freedom.

4. It is impossible to possess another person. If you do not possess your own self, it is equally hopeless to attempt to possess another.

You are here to learn and serve, and not to lord over others. You expand your omnipotence by the number of people you serve.

Take dominion over your thoughts and you are mightier than one who has taken a city.

Benefits of Principle Four

1. You are available to explore and enjoy the expanded you instead of trying to possess and control others.

2. You enjoy peace instead of aggression.

PRINCIPLE 5

Blame, the Destroyer of Personal Power

Whatever you blame becomes your superior. Grow your life by focusing on what is working in your life

In the bible is the story of the first man and woman and how they fell from grace. In that allegorical story, Adam and Eve, the first created people, were forbidden to eat of the tree of knowledge of good and evil. The wise snake in that wonderful garden of Eden, the habitat of our first ancestors, tempted Eve to eat of the fruit and she ate. She in turn suggested it to her husband who also ate of the fruit.

For disobedience, Almighty God sacked them from the glory of the garden of Eden. What is interesting in the story is how Adam quickly blamed his wife for tempting him and Eve quickly blamed it on the ancient serpent.

The story would have been different if Adam and Eve had accepted responsibility for their error and focused on how they could rectify the situation. By shifting the blame they each distanced themselves from the error and as such would not be able to learn from it for their growth.

Blame is the conscious surrendering and abuse of your power. Whatever you blame becomes your superior and remains so for as long as you blame it. What you blame binds you to the past through those you blame.

Even if you have been wronged, it is all right. You are not the first nor will you be the last to have this occur. There is none in life who has not been wronged. Being wronged in the past is no excuse for you to fail, suffer disease, or be robbed of your present happiness. "I was cheated, my uncles denied me support, I lost my father as a child, I was rejected by my parents." And so what? These same things have happened to everyone; and many have shown their light in darkness and risen to greatness. Stop the complaining and blaming; you are not going through anything new. No one stops you from what you can truly be. Only you can stop yourself.

In spite of being wronged, people have moved on to greater goodness. Those who have been wronged are doing the best they can with their lives right now. Only you are entitled to your feelings. The bad feelings are yours, not any one else's. Your bad feelings have the power to raise your blood pressure, cause palpitations, heart disease, weaken your immune system, blind you to present social and financial opportunities, make you suspicious and backward looking, and rob you of your happiness. You have no right to perpetrate such evil unto yourself. If you cannot love those who have wronged you, at least love yourself so much that you will not have time for them.

Blame gives you excuses and reasons to remain small, in lack, defeated, and limited. What excuses are you giving yourself to remain small, insignificant, and unnoticed? When you notice those excuses and false reasons and you dialogue with them, they will dissolve and you will be free to express greatness. Set standards of greatness and live by them. So, you see that in the allegorical story of Adam and Eve, it was not God who sacked them; it was the energy of blame that reduced them into insignificance and made them unworthy for the glorious garden.

People who blame are focusing on what must be done to them or for them and what must not be done to them or for them. They are always in the effect mode, because they focus on what others have caused them to feel. Whatever causes you to feel a certain way is your superior and you are an effect. Over time, you lose all your power to the external.

Some people blame their age for their inability to do something new that my lead them to greatness. A 45-year-old person may be ten times more intelligent than a 15-year-old person. In ten years from now, however, a 15-year-old lad could own a great business and command great wealth. This means that the 45-year-old person could achieve such wealthy ten times over in the same period of time. However, blame may keep the 45-year-old person in poverty while others prosper. No one has an excuse for failure.

Blame makes you focus on what is not working in your life and in so doing you energize and strengthen it, so what is not working gets worse. A useful alternative is to focus on what is working in your life and describe it with passion, then what is not working will begin to work. You have seen this in children at play. The one who is enthusiastic about his toy draws all the others to her side even if the others have more expensive toys than hers. If your marriage is not working, focus on and describe with passion what is working, such as your business, and the marriage will heal.

Each event in your life, painful or joyful, is meant to push you to higher spiritual grounds. It is only when you find the learning in the event that you quickly make that upward move. Life naturally moves in the direction of abundance. Therefore, nothing is depleted in the universe by your past error. There are still abundant opportunities for progress and happiness.

There is no standstill in life. There is either moving ahead or falling behind. You must make a decision to move forward and now is the time to do so. Don't allow yourself to get halted.

No man is infallible. Mistakes are normal and sometimes they produce pain. Let each pain in your life push you up to a higher vision. Your past misfortune has not and can never separate you from the good of life. There is only one life and one good. God is that goodness of the universe and you are a part of God.

You are here to be in dominion; that is your absolute destiny and life will never compromise on this. The earlier you decide to step into greatness, the better it is for you. In the allegorical story of Adam and Eve is the mention of the tree of life, guarded by angels so Adam and Eve may not go and eat of it and live. Blame is what blinds you from the tree of life; it stops you from living your life.

Set spiritual, social, psychological, physiological, and financial standards that you must live by and do not compromise them. Life is about increase, so it supports greatness. When you compromise a ton of what you value, life takes a hundred tons of it. When you compromise, you agree to go on a downward spiral and life pushes even faster down; that is what happens to all those who are descending.

Look deeply into what you blame and ask yourself, "What am I also responsible for?" Oh, yes, run this probe several times. If you did not cause your situation, you might have allowed it. You might have ignored internal and external warning signals. So, next ask yourself, "What did I allow?"

Once you identify how you caused or allowed your situation to happen, you can gently close your eyes, focus your attention at the solar plexus (the spot between the diaphragm and the navel) and with a passionate feeling say to yourself, *"I forgive myself for all the mistakes and confusions of the past. I love myself and I now move forward."*

Do this several times at one or two sittings until you feel the release and discover the learning in the blame.

How to Be Free from the Prison of Blame

1. Allow your eyes to close and make this statement several times. *"No one is responsible for my predicaments. I am responsible and I can change any predicament to joy."* You may substitute this statement with any that inspired you when you read through this principle.

2. As you make the statement listen to your life and notice what past events this is addressing.

3. When you find an event this statement is addressing, locate yourself at the beginning of that event. To be sure you are in that event, notice what you are seeing, hearing, tasting, smelling, and feeling. While in that event, make the statement several times. Look into the faces of the person or persons involved and make the statement.

4. Repeat the above three steps several times, allowing them to address other cuds or to stimulate abilities.

5. End your session by allowing your eyes to open.

There are also people who, fearing being blamed by someone, bend the rules of their personal comforts and do things they know are not necessary. These people are in effect practicing blame. They are going the unnecessary extra mile to please, thereby transferring their power to those they thought would blame them.

Most of the time, after bending so far backwards, they eventually realize their concerns are unfounded and the people they thought were expecting action or inaction from them are far removed from such expectations.

The human being is complex and you cannot know what anyone's expectations are. In any case, to try to please someone's expectations will turn you into a shapeless, purposeless amoeba. Be you and fulfill you for you. When you are fulfilled, all those around you experience the fulfillment and bless you for it.

Lessons on the Principle of Blame

1. What you blame rules over you.

2. Blame gives you an excuse and reason to remain small and insignificant.

3. Blame binds you to pain from your past and makes you vulnerable to attracting more pain into your life.

4. When instead of blame, you focus on what is working in your life, what is not working will transform and heal.

5. It is a sign of maturity to identify and accept your errors rather than to find something or someone to blame.

6. Blaming is running away from responsibility. You cannot run away from yourself. Your responsibility will sooner or later catch up with you.

Benefits of Principle Five

1. You live a responsible life.

2. You are a causative influence over life and you determine the effects you experience.

3. You are conscious of your actions and their effects and you manage them to your benefit.

PRINCIPLE 6
The Practice of Conscious Giving

Give to yourself; not to others and receive from no one except from life.

All of life is about giving. The sun gives sunlight for the plants to use in manufacturing food. We also take in all of the elements and food. In turn, we must give out as life gives. More important, we have to give out consciously. Whatever you keep in excess or hoard brings you pain. For example, to keep the water or the food in your body will produce disease. Everything you possess, such as land, property, and money, were once possessed by someone else. When it's your turn, you will eventually give it away. Conscious giving is to give with intention.

However, never give to anyone besides yourself. The sense of "I am giving away" creates a mental picture of losing your wealth. Those who give away eventually lack and they wonder why others do not give to them. True giving is giving into yourself. You give to increase the overflow of your joy in others. People lend you their life-fields to expand your joy through them. As such you are grateful for the opportunity to give someone. When you give with the idea of "I am becoming less in what I give," you will become less. Give with a mind of "I am giving to you to increase my joy." If your giving does not increase you, you threw it away to waste.

When you buy a product that you cherish you do not have a sense of becoming less. You have transmuted that money into an expanded joyful you. Giving is on the same principle; your giving must produce an expanded joyful you. So, in effect, you are giving into yourself. Every giving must expand some spiritual quality that you are.

The consciousness with which you give is very important. When giving is done with the consciousness to increase your joy or love through another, you give selflessly and abundantly. This is because no one thinks he is receiving too much. We want to have and have more abundantly; similarly, we must want to give and give abundantly. When your giving is to increase your joy through another, you are working magic. When parents give great joy to their child, their joy increases along with that of the child.

You are a spiritual energy field. When you sow your joy in this energy field you will surely harvest. Giving with a mind of increasing your joy compels life to give you everything you need to have great joy. You thus receive abundantly.

Avoid believing anyone is in need. To see people in need is to attract the consciousness of need. All people are extensions of you. To see a beggar or a person in need is to see a drain in yourself. Do not see a beggar to give to; see a field of opportunity to expand yourself into. Giving is of no value if it is not going to benefit the recipient. Often, you meet beggars on the wayside soliciting for alms. If you feel prompted to give to them, ask yourself if what you are giving will expand your consciousness. If not, your giving is a waste. When you conceive of yourself giving to a beggar or to people in need, you are reducing yourself, your wealth, and your consciousness. Giving is of no value if it does not benefit both the giver and recipient. To know if the giving will benefit the other person who is an extension of yourself, identify what virtue you are giving away. It is of benefit if it increases and strengthens. If the giving weakens the person by making him or her dependent on you this is not a blessing; you are creating dependants, or life suckers. In your giving, be sure you are increasing your well-being and becoming more independent in your whole self. When you give knowing that giving expands yourself in the other person, you give your best and it is always beneficial.

When you throw seeds on the farm, you grow them in yourself and for yourself because the harvesting is for you. The farm is different from you, yet it is an extension of you. Similarly, all people are extensions of you. When you give to expand you, the giving is devoid of fear. People are energy fields in which you grow the love, joy, health, and wisdom that you are. When you counsel someone to a great benefit, your wisdom grows in that person as well as in yourself. Enjoy it.

Never give what you have; give what you are. The money or property you give must represent the love, peace, health, or wisdom that you are. In so doing, your giving enriches you. When you give, it adds to you in someone else, so all giving must be done consciously to bring spiritual, social, psychological, financial, or physiological benefit to the recipient.

The story is told about one of my disciples who was hospitalized. The patient she shared the room with had pneumonia and they could not, therefore, use the air-conditioner to cool the room. Three weeks earlier, my disciple had gifted an electric fan to a friend. Interestingly, that friend happened to be working in the same hospital and had the opportunity to visit her. The young man saw her predicament and brought her that very electric fan to use. So, in effect she gave the fan to herself by gifting it to the other person.

Many who have come to understand the blessings of charity do not receive any blessings because, they do not give consciously. To give consciously is to give with intention to bring about growth, peace, or increase human abilities. If you are compelled or coerced into giving, you lose power, because the giving is not from you. It is from what compelled you to give.

Giving is not only about money. It is about anything you release from you to benefit another with no expectation whatsoever that it will benefit you in return. It includes the giving of your time, service, prayer, counseling, or smile.

Giving opens you to receive, because in giving you trust in the abundance of the universe. With that focus you attract abundance to you. You must, however, not give with a mind of receiving. If you do, it will be tantamount to manipulation. The sun gives out its energy without expecting anything back. Expecting to receive holds in itself deep fear of what might happen if you do not receive. It will narrow your attention to you; and if you happen to be in some difficulty, your attention on that difficulty will attract more of that to you. You must give to increase life. Your attention should be on how your giving will bring blessings to the recipient.

Also, an attitude of non-giving is based in an attitude of fear. Deep behind non-giving is the fear of lack. "If I give and I am sick I will not have money to support myself." "If I give, when I grow old I will be poor and miserable." Eventually, people attract the experiences they fear unto themselves, because subconsciously they are focusing on the fear. Giving with fear focuses you on the experience of lack. Fearless giving is trust in the abundance of life. That trust focuses you on life's abundance and thus brings abundance to you.

Rich and successful people have a conscious giving program. Your giving must reflect your income. If a person tithes $20 a month, the person is affirming that her value is $200 a month. Whatever the person is earning in excess of $200 can be perceived as stealing.

Overruns and Dependents

When something happens repeatedly in life it calls for study and a search for solution. There is this phenomenon I call "over-run." When you overly give to somebody for a long time, and the person is not able to give back to you, the person tends to hate you or becomes your competitor or rival. Many people who have raised their siblings or friends realize to their dismay that those they helped are undermining them or ignoring them, especially when they have also risen to some degree of success. This phenomenon is what I call over-run. You over-run the person you previously gave to.

In giving, you may create a dependant person or an over-run; both situations destroy your giving. When you give to expand your consciousness in and through other persons, your giving provides them with increased and enlarged consciousness and results in peace and respect. To become an over-run is dangerous as it leads you into ingratitude. Ingratitude to life makes your life a struggle.

Two rich women heard of the spiritual benefits of giving. The first person built food houses, went to the streets and gathered all the poor and brought them in and fed them. The second year, she went to the streets and found twice as many more poor people. She brought them in and fed them. She did the same for the third and fourth years, bringing in twice as many more poor people to be fed. She eventually ran out of resources and died and went to heaven. On a scale of one to one hundred, where one hundred is the highest, she was placed on a scale of five. The second rich woman built factories for the disabled and the weak. She went to the streets and gathered all the poor and brought them in and gave each one a job to do according to his or her ability. Out of their work, she earned profit. The second year, she went to the streets and brought in a few more poor people. She gave them employment and made profits from their labor. The neighborhood considered this rich woman a mean person who exploited the poor. She eventually died and went to heaven. On a scale of one to one hundred, where one hundred is the highest, she was placed on a scale of ninety-five. She received her high grade because she created independent beings.

Your giving must foster spiritual independence and growth of creativity. Never give to create a sense of dependency in people.

Give to a creative medium of life and all of life goes to work for you. A creative medium is any ministry that is working to produce love, joy, and peace on earth. It is whatever you consider is doing the highest good on earth. Your church, or a community organization regardless of size, may be that medium.

Receiving from Life

There are people who are great givers but poor receivers, which is equally dangerous. They are denying themselves the benefits that life insists all must receive. Giving must be complemented by receiving. The principle of receiving demands that you receive only from life and not from individuals.

To receive rightly, therefore, is to receive from no one except life. No one can truly give to you but life. Each person is a channel through which life fulfills its duties to another. When you see your donors as the hands of life to meet your need, you are always available to receive from them and from other sources. It is no shame to receive from life, so there will be no need to grow into an over-run person. Receive from no one and your gratitude to life will bless the channels through which life gave to you, who will in turn see you as an ever fertile soil to grow new seeds of love, beauty, and joy.

When you see life as the giver, you are open to receive from it through any of her numerous channels. If you create fixed receiving points you become an exploiter or reduce yourself into a beggar. If any of the fixed points does not give you what you are expecting, you are likely to generate negative thoughts in your mind and those thoughts reduce you. If you receive from individuals instead of from life, you will experience inner resistance to receive more from the same person. If you have to go to the same person again you begin to fabricate lies as to the reasons for your needs and those lies will reduce you.

Think of the lies and pretense you employ when you want to receive something from someone. Although it may be given from the heart of goodness, it is received with a heart full of lies, pretense, and guilt. The heart with which you receive is what you truly receive. Your receiving will manifest the evils of the lies, pretense, and guilt with which it was received.

When you receive with a sense of guilt, the receiving will become a curse. When you receive from the same person several times you begin to feel guilty. When you receive from life through any channel, there is no sense of guilt. Life has a responsibility to take care of itself as you and does so through her chosen channels; and that vessel can be just one person.

When you receive and bless life as the giver, the all-ness of life blesses the channel. Then the channel, through receiving more, may continue to give to you. No one gives; only life gives. So receive from life.

In each moment you are giving and receiving material, mental, and emotional products. The wave pattern of your thoughts and feeling are available for all to receive and use. Others may pick up your thoughts though you have never met them, and act upon them. Be conscious of the thoughts you are putting into the environment by asking yourself, "Will the thoughts and feelings I am now giving to the world produce peace, love, and joy for those who will receive them?" Such a practice lifts you above ordinary human living.

A Practice of Giving

In practicing giving, the first and only person to give to is yourself. You are not the body sculpture that you wear. You are a spirit being living with a mind, feelings, and a body. Each of these aspect is an intelligent field in itself. These aspects are interconnected and may exist independent of each other. Practice giving to your mind, feelings, and body.

In the story of the birth of Jesus, three wise men presented him with the gifts of gold, frankincense, and myrrh.

1. Gold is usually found mixed up in rock particles. It has to be ground, mixed with chemicals, then extracted. It represents the evolved state of the mind that has been freed from all base human thoughts. To give to your mind, acknowledge the perfect state of the mind and describe it until it is real to you. Probe into yourself, "When I am mentally evolved, what is that like?"

Respond to this enquiry several times until you know it to be true.

2. The frankincense speaks of the evolved state of feeling. Frankincense has a deodorizing fragrance. There are people whose presence in an argument adds fuel to the fire. There are others who generate soothing and healing feelings; these are those who have an evolved feeling body. When you go to a room where people have just quarreled, you feel the energy of tension. Similarly, a person whose presence inspires soothing feelings can be felt. Probe into yourself, "When I am emotionally evolved, what is that like?" Respond to this enquiry several times until you know it to be true.

3. Myrrh arrests degeneration. It is, therefore, used to mummify the dead to arrest decomposition. It speaks of the evolved, ever-rejuvenated physical state. Probe into yourself, "When I am physically evolved, what is that like?" Respond to this enquiry several times until you know it to be true.

The three-step practice above invites the attention of your spirit to the various aspects, or bodies. Wherever the spirit rests, there is healing. Respond to the enquiries in each of the steps above several times in meditation and you will bring out the perfection in your bodies. You cannot give what you do not have. Self charity enriches you and enables you to give to your extended self in others.

An Expanded Giving Program

If giving opens one to receive, this giving practice will open you to receive abundantly.

A thought produces arousal. Ask yourself, "What other thought in me can produce healing, marital harmony, joy, love, peace, or financial abundance?"

The next practice is to expand your giving to enrich others, knowing that they are your extensions. To do this, follow the three steps below.

1. Identify thoughts that can bring you joy, health, creativity, or whatever you desire. Nurse and celebrate those thoughts, and let their energy fill you.

2. Identify who needs that thought and its feeling.

3. Identify the thoughts the person needs in order to stimulate the feeling.

The three steps may be summarized thus: What thoughts can bring me joy? Who needs this joy? What thoughts in this person can produce joy in him or her? Be aware that the thought bringing you joy may be that of a financial increase of $2.5 billion. This same thought in someone else may cause him or her to faint. The thought for another person to have the same joy may be the thought of reconciling with his ex-wife, so that will be the thought you have to hold for him. While feeling your joy as in step one, connect to the spirit of the other person by asking, "What thought in 'James' can produce a similar joy?" You will discern what thought James needs in order to feel the quality of joy you are feeling. Hold James in that thought. For example, you may hold the thought that says, "James, you are reconciled with your ex-wife." By this process you have released that thought to James and that is a great gift. You may expand yourself into a universal giver by probing for what thoughts in all mankind will bring about world peace and then hold all mankind in it.

In practice, for each month of the year, identify two or more gifts you gave out consciously and two or more gifts received. When you focus on the gifts you gave out you open your tap for more of universal good to flow through; and when you focus on the gifts you received, you open yourself to have more. The true giver is Spirit; by focusing on the gifts that have streamed through you, you widen the door of your soul through which the gifts came. Focusing on the gifts you received opens you to appreciation; and when you appreciate a gift, the donor feels like giving more. Therefore, by focusing on the gifts you received, you open yourself to receive more. By reading this list daily to yourself or meditating on the gifts you gave out or received, you reconnect, or "re-member," yourself with the goodness of life.

Lessons on the Principle of Conscious Giving

1. Giving is the act of expanding the good you are.

2. He who gives to the poor is made poor because he focuses on poverty; he who receives in a mindset of needing, lacks.

3. Give to what you are in all people.

4. Consciously give to feed your mind, feelings, and body.

5. What you give consciously is never lost; it creates an energy field for you to enjoy.

6. When you expect a reward from your giving, it is manipulation.

7. Be available to receive only from Life.

8. Life is an expansion of you. Therefore, giving is an act of enriching yourself.

9. It is Life who gives and Life changes the channels of giving as it sees to be divinely right. So never expect from a source you have chosen.

Benefits of Principle Six

1. Giving expands and enriches you.

2. Giving creates a world that is meaningful and loving to all.

3. Receiving is spiritual surrender to the good that Life seeks to do.

PRINCIPLE 7
The Practice of Conscious Change

Grow with change.

Change is inevitable and is happening always. When embraced early, it occurs in joy. When delayed, it comes with pain. Something is always seeking to give birth to itself in every moment. There is no standstill in life. There is either moving ahead or falling behind.

Each moment you are changing. In fact, you are not the same person you saw or knew a moment ago. Even in your body, moment by moment, old cells are dying and new ones are being born. You are like a kaleidoscopic field of shimmering colors, changing each moment.

Without the force of change, life is impossible. Without change you would have remained an egg in your mother's womb. Without change life would be so dull and ineffective that it would demand change.

To fight against what is inevitable is to experience pain. Embrace change and celebrate life. Embrace the newness that change brings in each moment. Review and gracefully surrender attitudes that do not serve you.

Do not allow yourself to be unconscious of the changes that are occurring in you. Participate in your own life; you have a say in what changes within you and what it changes into. It is what you are changing from and into that is important and that requires your conscious input. Decide what your body, mind, or feelings are changing from and into.

Changes in Relationships

Most hurts in life occur in relationships: hurts and pains from a husband, wife, boyfriend, and others. Nothing is static or stationary. Life is like dancing mercury; flow with it. Whatever is happening is for a reason or a season. Relationships may break when their season or reason is over. You go through pain because you may still be holding on to what is seeking its release. The partner who leaves the relationship believes he or she has done what is best for him or her. It is you who is holding on to the thinking of hurt. The moment you realize you are holding on to the relationship in your thinking, you can let go of it. Each person is on an authentic journey of self-discovery and you cannot stop it.

Life has given you 6.5 billion people on the planet to explore. You probably have not yet met but a tiny fraction of them, so you do not have the justification to ruin your life just because one person decided to leave your life. It is possible that ten times the joy you are experiencing in this relationship is awaiting you in another relationship. Do not stop yourself from loving again. Every day has its freshness. Love again as though it never hurt before.

Many who hold on to relationships that have technically ended are afraid of loneliness. Here relationships include the ones you have with your parents, children, and others. Some parents are attached to their children so much that they fear their leaving home. You may have to live alone but that does not necessarily make you lonely unless you choose to be lonely. Loneliness is when you cut yourself off from the magic of life. Being alone is an opportunity to explore more without hindrance of a partner's opinion. Sometimes a break in a relationship is a way life frees you to be more you and to be available for you.

The fear of loneliness makes some people accept abuse in a relationship. The more you allow yourself to receive abuse, the more you reduce your value and presence. So you eventually lose that relationship and the chance of creating new ones.

When you are an emotional and mental wreck, your partner has good reason to gleefully walk away. Again, when you reduce yourself into an emotional and mental wreck, your partner may manipulate you to boost his or her ego. He knows that no matter how inhumanly he treats you, whenever he comes back, you will accept him so he will walk in and out as he pleases. When you see that the relationship is over, accept it and gracefully move on. Others fear that if the person in their life leaves, no one else will come into their lives. When you do such mental computation, you create that experience in your life. No relationship is meant to last forever. Every relationship will end one day, at least through death. Even if you were to die together, there is no guarantee that you will walk the same spiritual road in the next life. There are infinite numbers of opportunities for fresh relationships. For example, a woman lives in Ghana, a man from China comes on holiday, falls in love with her, and they get married. The possibilities are endless. When your partner says no to you, do not say no to yourself. Affirm what you are, embrace change, and move on.

The Power of Changing Your Mind

You have the wonderful gift of change; use it to change your mind, feelings, or body. It is okay to change your mind. Review your life; look at what thoughts might be producing your experiences. If the experiences are not what you like, simply go to the beginning of that thought and say, "I change my mind," and add what you are changing it into. The steps are as follows:

1. State the thought that is no longer serving your need.

2. State what you are changing it into.

3. State the results you expect.

When you wake up each morning, notice what you are and determine what you are changing into. Watch the changes occurring in your life. Soon change will happen according to what you determine.

Change, the Inevitable

If change were not an integral part of your life, you would remain in your mother's womb. Even as you are reading this, you are changing. Life is constantly changing; the earth is changing through erosion, earthquakes, stormy rains, and all of life's processes. The old must transmute into new life and new life emerges from the old. Flow with the progressive currents of life, gracefully surrendering old outmoded thoughts and attitudes.

Greet yourself each day as a new wonderful soul. You may not understand all of the changes happening in you and around you. That is because change may take you down unfamiliar roads. Embrace change, look into its face, and ask, "What is seeking to show itself here?"

Change is inevitable, but you have the right to determine what you change into. To determine what you are changing into, you must know what you are changing from, what caused the change, and the reasons to change into something else. Adjust along with the change into a new and wonderful being, revealing more of the image and likeness of your Creator. Celebrate the obstacles you are going through right now, for they are pushing you out of the shell of your mortal egg into a larger dimension than you can dream of. The unborn chick may find the circumference of its shell to be huge and wonderful. Think of what it finds when it breaks out of its shell and sees the new horizon. When you embrace change, it births you into a larger horizon.

Who has ever dreamt that the ugly caterpillar will one day become a most beautiful butterfly? Such beautiful things often have what to the human senses appear as queer beginnings. The stages of change of the caterpillar to the butterfly speak of what is happening in our individual lives. Trust the process of life to change you from glory to glory. The occasional pains we experience may be likened to a woman in labor. The pain is the birthing of a new generation. Let this be your realization: *"I am the being changed into the greater beauty, power and likeness of God. It is not a bad situation; I am being transformed into...* (state the positive and powerful)."

Fear of Change

Many people are afraid of change, because they are not sure what the future holds for them. In truth, people are not afraid of the future. You cannot fear what you do not know. You are afraid of losing what you are accustomed to. What you are used to is changing constantly; and if you do not change consciously with change, you eventually lose what you are accustomed to. Fear of change gives birth to attachment to things and situations in life, and this stalls growth.

People want to experience some new progress in their lives, yet they are afraid to initiate the needed changes that will produce it. If you want different results you must consciously identify what you are doing and where that is taking you, then initiate new actions to produce the desirable result. The steps are as follows:

1. Notice old results

2. Identify the cause of the old results

3. Identify the desired results

4. Focus on what change is needed in order to produce the desired results

You cannot expect different results if you persist in your old ways; you must change. Change is already happening; harvest its energy and direct it to your goal.

Re-starting Life

Change sometimes means starting all over and it is okay to do so. There is newness in every moment and newness holds the magic of original creative ideas. In the water cycle the water that flows downstream rises up as water vapor and falls back as rain into the places where the water started. If life invites you to cycle to the beginning, be open to it. Many who resist this call to change waste their precious life in stagnancy.

Many great beginnings are the results of people coming to an end of their comfort zone. Life is advancing its own self and may crush what you are accustomed to in order to provide you with fresh beginnings for your higher good. You may have several examples of misfortunes that turned out to be blessings. For example, a person is laid off or fired. Many see this as an end to life as they know it. They focus on the fears that come from not having a steady flow of income. They obsess over bills and the possibility of losing their home when in essence it is an opportunity to begin something new and have a better life.

Starting all over again may require you to go back to school or receive some other form of education and training. It is a necessary investment of time.

Growing Old and Aging Old

When you were young, you were eager to grow and let the world know you were mature. Some even inflate their ages so others will believe they are mature. Then comes age forty and they begin to be afraid of what old age may bring. They resist growth and start to age. Fear creates obstacles to their future.

There are people who actually feel sad when they get to their forties. They do not want others to know they are forty because they are not accepting change. Yes, I agree that age is only a number and a state of consciousness. However, when higher age means an increase in all mental, spiritual, and material resources and the enjoyment of the buoyancy of great health, all will want to reveal their ages. You cannot hide behind metaphysical jargon. Check your reasons for not telling your age, especially when you are around forty years old and above. Your mind knows the secret fears you have and attracts experiences in accordance with them. Plan consciously to grow old, seasoned with vibrant health and mental acumen.

When you change with change, you grow. When you resist change, you age. There is a great difference between growing old and aging old. To grow is to increase, expand, and be more; and as you increase in age consciously, you are able to do more with less effort. To grow old, therefore, is to increase in your mental and emotional abilities. It means you are able to achieve more in less time and with less energy. Many resist old age. There is nothing wrong with old age if you grow into it; the problem arises when you age into it. Those who age old, wither, fade, and degenerate with age. African teaching states, "The adult who is grown is mightier than a prophet." This teaches that there are adults who have aged but not grown.

Get out of the race consciousness; old age does not necessarily mean sickness and death. Death is imperative and may come at any time; even the sun will one day die and new suns will be born. Life is here with you now; enjoy it. The dawning sun is beautiful, so is the noontime sun; and the setting sun is magical to watch. Similarly, practicing conscious change, you plan for a magical ending; making it a joyous twilight for others to watch and say, "A life arose beautifully and is set in magic and magnificence."

Let us also look at it this way: from age one to forty you are exploring life. At age forty, you are mature because you have gone through adventure, experimentations, and explorations and you know what you really want. Truly, then, life begins at forty. Your life has just begun; you know the seeds to plant into a glorious future. You know what works for your health, finances, and social well being. Pause at age forty and identify the seeds you have gathered for your well being. What have you been so far and what do you intend for the rest of your days? The play is not over at age forty and above. Only the style of the game may change and that is romantic. With all of the wrinkles and gray hair, every age has its own beauty. Just as the flowers in the spring are beautiful, so are the plants in winter when snow falls on them.

People fear of old age because they do not plan to grow into it. We plan to grow our business; similarly, we need to plan to grow our lives with time. When you plan to grow your mental abilities with the passage of time, you will know what mental and emotional exercises to initiate. In African life and philosophy, old age is synonymous with wisdom. The old are consulted in all major affairs; they are venerated and celebrated by their children and grandchildren and by the community. Making old age synonymous with degeneration is an agreement that causes aging. Loving to grow old with positive expectancy grows you into celebration. Embrace the increase of your days and let each day be the increase of your wisdom. As we grow old, we gain knowledge and as such our energy shifts from muscular force and abilities to the mental. It is, therefore, important to engage in programs, such as reading, recalling and writing about your joyful youthful days, and playing crosswords or any other game that stimulates the mind and keeps it active.

Enjoy your youthful memories; step into your youthful days in your mind and enjoy this time of life fully in youthfulness. Bring all the glories and inheritance you acquired with you. You do not have to leave all the good of your youth and pine away. Get involved with children, play games with them, teach them and learn their ways. In a way, children are your seniors because they are born in a time when the earth was older and more experienced than when you were born.

What you are today is the sum total of all the thoughts, feelings, and actions of the past. Your past, however cannot determine your present and your future. There is a spiritual you that is bigger and mightier then your past. This spiritual you can determine your future irrespective of what your past ha been. You have the right to go into your yesterdays and cha the images and thus change your present. You can determine your future today through change.

How to Grow Consciously with Change

Respond to these soul prompts listed below as fast as you can. Do not think about them. Let the answers flow spontaneously from your spirit. As you progress, the flow of the answers will be more spontaneous. Do this with your eyes closed.

1. What and where am I in Time, Energy, Space, and Circumstance, and why?

2. Where do I want to be in Time, Energy, Space, and Circumstance, and why?

3. Respond to steps one and two several times, allowing these steps to address other cuds or to stimulate abilities.

4. End your session by allowing your eyes to open.

As you do these steps, answers will flow from your inner soul to nourish you.

A further practice is to consciously remember your yesterdays, past weeks, and months. This practice develops within you the power to pass through life consciously.

Be Conscious of Newness

Noticing what is new is a magical process. It brings you into now and opens you up for fresh inputs from life. A useful practice is to describe what in your body, your spouse's body, children, parents, your surroundings, and in life that is different from the way it was in the past. No two days are alike and you are not the same in two successive moments. You are changing moment by moment, so notice what is new and beautiful in you today that is different from how it was yesterday.

1. What is new and beautiful in today that is different from how it was yesterday and all of the days in the past?

2. What is new and good that is happening to my life now?

3. What is new and beautiful in your body which is different from how it was yesterday and all of the days in the past?

Expand the probe to embrace your workmates or schoolmates, your community, and the elements. What is new and beautiful in the weather today that is different from how it was yesterday and all of the days in the past?

Lessons on the Principle of Change

1. Change is inevitable and is happening always. When embraced early, it occurs in joy. When delayed, it comes with pain.

2. You have a say in what change you must experience in life, so participate in the process consciously.

3. Do not allow yourself to be unconscious of the change that is occurring in you.

4. Change is an opportunity for a deeper exploration of life.

5. It is okay to change your mind. It is what you change it from and to and the result of that change that is important, and this must be determined by you.

6. Everything is for a reason or for a season. When the reason or the season is over, change must occur and must be embraced with dignity.

7. You can choose to grow old and not age old.

8. Loneliness is not when you are alone. It is when you cut yourself from the magic and self expansion that life offers.

9. To grow is to expand in capabilities and be more.

10. Change offers, growth, regeneration, renewal, and freshness. You have the right to determine what to change to.

You have the right to change yourself into a new you now.

Be excited about change instead of fearing change because change is your ally for your highest good.

Benefits of Principle Seven

1. You become dynamic and adventurous and you realize that life is fun.

2. Change keeps you stable and steadfast.

3. You learn to surrender easily and gracefully what needs to be surrendered.

4. You exercise your power to determine the outcome of change.

5. When you are in stride with change and determining the outcome, you are ahead of your peers.

6. When you are in stride with change the forces of Time, Energy, Space and Circumstance heed your call.

7. Energy is never lost. You can go into your past and claim all of the energies you should have used before and you can bring them into your present state.

PRINCIPLE 8
The Practice of Conscious Gratitude

Celebrate the Magic called Life.

We have said "Thank you" from childhood to the extent that it is automatic and has no energy.

Gratitude is the conscious recognition of the wonderment that is happening and the awareness of how that wonderment benefits you. Gratitude is to acknowledge with thankfulness the benefits received from someone– this time from life. Given with a clear vision of the good, gratitude moves the benefactor to give more of that good, and makes you worthy of receiving more goodness. You experience more of what you are grateful for. Showing gratefulness to a benefactor opens you to receive greater help.

Life is magical, spontaneous, and present. To see this wonderment is to be wonderful. Be magical by seeing the magic in life. Life has become another human person you may communicate intelligibly with – that's magical. Life has become 6.5 billion people on the planet for your companionship. For a grain of corn to blossom into a stalk of corn, all of life comes together, supplying many inputs for that to happen – that's magical. Birds, fish, and flowers of various colors and shades are available for our sight to enjoy. The ability to hear, taste, smell, feel, and see; the orchestrated harmony of the organs of the body to maintain balance; all of these and many more speak of the wonderment of life. Conscious practice of gratitude makes you focus on the good and takes you out of pain and complaints. You realize that great things are happening just for you and what you may complain about is insignificant. Life has outdone itself for our complete joy. Your very presence and being is magical and makes complaining a blasphemy and a desecration of your life. Gratitude is participation in the magic of life. Each moment something new is happening as the people you meet, the elements that greet you, and the life forms you enjoy. You do not see the same person twice and no condition is repeated. Life is constantly new, and it is all happening just for you.

Gratitude is the:

Most powerful energy for transformation on the planet.

Christ conscious state of "I have recognized the good."

Audible or inaudible "thank you" that you say to life or to someone.

Gratitude is the accepted and accomplished state. It is the state of the "it is done" experience. The master Jesus advised that when you pray, believe you have received and you will receive. What he was teaching is that you pray from the accomplished state – the state of gratitude. When you pray from anxiety, the results of that prayer, even if fulfilled, are colored with anxiety. When you pray from the place of gratitude, the results are colored with joy and love, which are the energies of gratitude. Gratitude is the key that opens the door to the greater treasures of life. Gratitude moves you to the end result of every need or prayer. It is, therefore, the highest form of prayer.

Whether you believe in God or not, a scientific observation of life tells you that there is an intelligent purposefulness behind the universe. This intelligence has various names. Whether you call it by a name or not, this intelligent life deserves your constant gratitude.

Don't wait for God to do what He/She has given you the power to do. "Why worry when you can create? God has invested and vested himself as you and that calls for an everlasting gratitude."

A story is told in the Bible of Jesus healing ten people and only one of them returned to say thank you. Jesus wondered why the other nine had not come to show gratitude. When I was young I used to think Jesus was on an ego trip, seeking the gratitude of men. The truth is that the spirit of gratitude accentuates perfect healing. The man who is in the spirit of gratitude escapes sin because he is focused on good. When you make gratitude a moment by moment exercise, you become powered by so much good that evil cannot find room in your life. Evil finds room in the heart of the man who does not have gratitude. Jesus knew that if the other nine did not find gratitude in their hearts, they would reopen themselves to evil and they would be vulnerable to some other disease.

Gratitude opens you to the goodness of life. For example, if someone gives you a gift and sees you using it wisely, the person feels happy and thinks of giving you more. The universe is watching for your signs of gratitude and simply opens greater doors to you.

Gratitude places you in a place of constant receiving of the good you have recognized. Gratitude always speaks of your recognition of the good, and recognizing the good opens you to experience greater good. Capture this idea: by recognizing the good, your attention is focused on the good and you continue to experience more of the quality or color of that good. Consciously look for the good in life.

The law of the mind is that it merges or becomes one with what it focuses on. The man who is filled with gratitude is the one who is always focusing on something good. Gratitude makes you focus on the good and thus opens the portals of your life to experience greater good.

Attention is the direction of your energy to an idea or object. Whatever receives your attention receives healing. Gratitude brings you into the now. It brings your attention to the object that receives your praise and when that object is a part of your body, business, or aspirations, the object of praise receives healing or empowerment.

Gratitude makes you focus on what is working in your life. Then what is not working in your life will begin to work also.

When you see something joyful, you feel joyful. Gratitude makes you see what to be joyful for and the joy you feel heals your body and stimulates visions of possibilities.

A life of gratitude is a life of perpetual joy. Gratitude contains in itself the ability to dissolve past pains and presents to you the fullness of the moment. Gratitude opens your eyes to see the great wonders happening in your life right here and now. It takes you from the past or the future and gives you the fullness of the present moment to enjoy.

Gratitude is not meant for good times only; gratitude is choosing to focus on the good in spite of the seeming evil around you. You may also focus on the good you expect to come and be grateful.

Thank you, God, for the pain, trouble, or misfortune and for the great good my life is unfolding to be through that pain.

In every event, ask yourself, *"What good can come out of this for which I am to be grateful to life or to Father-Mother God?"* Viewing events in this way lifts you above the pain and human conditions. Another approach is to realize, *"Even as the light comes out of darkness, some good is about to emerge out of this pain."* You do not overcome disease. Everything is a part of God. You cannot use God to destroy an aspect of God. Lift the disease to its glory in gratitude. Your attitude should be, *"Glory of God in this disease, show forth your glory now!"*

You have to separate your behaviors from yourself. Your action or attitude may have been wrong, but that does not make you a wrong manifestation of God. God has not made a mistake in creating you. "God believes in you just as you are."

For you to be alive today, you must be filled with gratitude. Ingratitude is to say that Life has not been life to you and that is a negation of the goodness that life is towards you and of what life is doing as you.

All challenges and successes have been magnificently rewarded with lessons. Even if the challenge threw you into darkness, you had the opportunity to see the stars, which could not be viewed under the bright sun. The stars then are symbolic of greater opportunities to explore.

Devote your life to seeing the beauty in life. It is a practice that makes you joyful and the light of joy inspires love, vibrant health, and a drive for excellence. The lack of the vision of what is beautiful makes you a mournful seeker in life. Then each day becomes droll, meaningless, and without purpose. Each day is like the previous one.

If you are faced with a conflict or quarrel, pause, close your eyes, and declare one to three good things about your opponent before you speak. If possible, declare the good you know about your adversary to his hearing before you become caught up in the conflict. Jesus taught, "Agree with your adversary quickly."

When you see the good in your brother and declare it, you have linked with his higher nature. You then achieve two things:

- You awaken more of the good in him.
- You merge with the good you see, thus making you shine with each goodness.

A Way to Practice Gratitude

There are three components of gratitude:

- Who you are grateful to.
- What you are grateful for.
- The reason for gratitude or the benefit you derived from the good done to you.

1. Using the three components of gratitude, list things you have not prayed or asked for but are provided and upon which you depend. Write in the form of " I am grateful to — for doing — for me, which has brought me — blessings."
2. Using the three components of gratitude, list things that have happened to you for which you are grateful. Do your writing as directed in step one.

3. Read these lists to yourself daily. Find ten things to be grateful for in each day and read the list to yourself as you fall asleep and when you wake up in the morning.

Celebrate Failure

A mistake is an error unrealized. When an error is realized, it is no more a mistake; it is a learning or discovery. You have discovered a way or ways that do not work. This discovery calls for gratitude and celebration. Often we never celebrate our mistakes. Our memory, therefore, is clouded with the error and not the learning we received from it. When your mind is filled with memories of mistakes and pain, it attracts similar situations to you. You thus stop yourself from consistent success.

1. To correct this, list all of the mistakes you have made in life.

2. For each of these mistake, state the lesson or strength you received from it.

3. State how useful that lesson has been.

Gratitude and Blessing

Gratitude goes with blessing. To bless is to release the energy of good to someone or to a condition. Blessing is a two-step process.

1. You activate a positive feeling. This is done by recalling what you have to be grateful for.

2. You release that joy to one who needs it.

The good you bless increases and the evil you bless loses its power to harm. Gratitude is a state of living in perpetual blessing.

Lessons on the Principle of Gratitude

1. Gratitude is the highest of all spiritual practices.

2. There is so much to be grateful for in life.

3. When you see the magic in life you ignite the magic that you are.

4. Gratitude is the key that opens the door to greater riches of life.

5. There is healing in gratitude; it has the power of multiplication of good and is a transforming energy.

Benefits of Principle Eight

1. Gratitude keeps you poised, positive, and passionate about life.

2. It heals and immunizes you to pain.

3. It increases your good.

4. It opens your consciousness for more opportunities for growth.

5. Gratitude realigns you with spirit and energizes you with all possibility. It enhances your creativity.

PRINCIPLE 9
Purposeful Living

Identify and expand what you are for nothing is yours except what you are.

A life without purpose is like a ship without a guide and destination. It will be blown by any wind to any direction. Your life must not be such a random, wasteful event. True purpose is what your goals and achievements are fulfilling. It is the divine idea of God about your life. You can, therefore, only know it from God.

Here is a simple question. Its true answer will give you a vision and meaning for your life, and transform it for you.

"A time comes, which we call it death, when you realize that nothing in this world is yours except what you are. What are you?"

When that time comes, you realize that your spouse, parents, children and friends is not yours; your properties and estates are not yours; and in fact, your own body is not yours. All that is yours is what you are. What are you?

Your personal answer to the above questions makes you focus on what matters. It makes you respect the body and all of the possessions you have. How is what you are doing today establishing and expanding what you are? How is what you have and value enlarging what you are? Everything you have was once someone else's possession. It is now your turn to use it to expand what you are.

What is your purpose? What you are is the purpose and the reason for your being here. Permit yourself to express the highest and the best in every aspect of your life.

Your purpose will free you from the trappings of the world. Everything must be fulfilling something in your life or be released to circulate to the one who needs it. This enables you to escape wasteful living.

Truly, this world has nothing that you really need. You are all the world needs to fulfill itself – that is why it called for you; and you responded by coming to earth. You are an answer to life's prayer. Be willing to express the treasures that you are.

Look at life. What do you see? Life is moving in the direction of love, abundance, and joy; and so are you. What are you in this vast field we call life?

Give yourself the space to stimulate the answers in silence. When you know what you are as a spirit being, life will unfold its purpose. You are already loaded and coded with the substance of divine goodness. All you have to do is to promote and expand what you are. When you invite people to your party, they come to enjoy what you are and not what you have, such as the food, drink, or music. People need to learn to be available for life to celebrate what they are. Through the life you live, life experiences fullness. Be conscious of the life you live, and of its purpose and value.

Have a Dream Bigger Than You. If your dream is not bigger than you, then your life is not worth living. And if you cannot do big things, do small things in big ways.

You are here to expand and be more. A big dream demands that you step out of your comfort zone and be more. It is uncomfortable to remain small. Your joy increases as you expand. Dream of the impossible and ask yourself, "Why not?"

Everything in life was once impossible until someone asked, "In what ways can it be done?" Achieve the impossible and let it expand what you are.

Enter into dialogue with each day and let it reveal its purpose to you. Each day is a whole new array of possibility. Therefore, ask each day to tell you what magic of God it is to be for you. Remember that you cannot determine your purpose or the purpose for each day; purpose already is. Purpose is the magic; it is the knowing of the intent of the universe for your life. Purposeful living places you in oneness with God, with life, and with the infinite goodness that is ever flowing. Life is a self-sustaining, self-maintaining, perfectly balanced order. Purpose cannot be anything other than what life already is. Other life forms support the perfect balance of your life and your life supports other life forms as well. You are a sounded note in the great musical orchestra and you are a very important one.

A Way to Purposeful Living

You cannot know your purpose. You have to ask it from your creator. Every manufacturer has a purpose for its product and specifications for the product. The relationship between you and God is more than that of a manufacturer and manufactured products. You are an extension of God. Ask God to give you the specifications for Itself as you.

Your purpose must determine who your wife or husband must be. When you pray to God saying, "Give me a good wife or husband," God will reply, "I created all people in my image and likeness, so they are all equal and none is bad." The ideal way to choose a mate is to identify your purpose and seek the person whose purpose naturally supports yours, and vice versa.

You cannot know your purpose through the logical mind. Your logical mind calculates things from its history and nothing of your history can tell what your purpose must be. Your purpose is established in your spirit. The following exercise, done daily, will open you to the voice of your spirit and you will know your purpose. With knowing comes universal support for its accomplishment.

In silent contemplation, respond to this soul enquiry several times.

"A time comes, which I call death, when I realize that nothing in this world is mine except what I am. What am I?"

How is what I have now affirming and expanding what I am? What is God as God through me? What is God's awareness of itself as me? What is God's idea of today for my life?

Responding to the above prompts in silence will open the glory of the day to you.

Your purpose takes you into the original proverbial Eden. This is the eating of the fruit of life.

Before a meeting, ask, "What is God's idea of this participant in this meeting?" This question leads you into conscious purposeful living.

Purpose is not your goals. Purpose is what your goals are to achieve in your life.

"Ye are the light of the world." When you are the light of the world, what problem can you have with darkness?

Practice One

List all of your possessions. These include your physical assets, such as eyes, ears, and hands, as well as your material possessions, such as houses and cars.

How are my possessions supporting what I am? Dialogue with your possessions. Ask them what they are here to accomplish. Knowing what your beauty or handsomeness is to accomplish; what your cars, wife, friends, and children are to accomplish in your life, helps you to awaken to what you are here to accomplish in life.

When you know your purpose, you will realize that there is no place in life for mediocrity. You are the marvel and miracle of life. God has come to its own self as you. You are the celebration of life. You are not to pass through life unnoticed. You are the exclamation of life's glory.

Lessons on the Principle of Purposeful Living

1. You must fulfill the reason you are here.
2. An unexamined life is not worth living.
3. Life has a purpose that includes you in its scheme of events.

Benefits of Principle Nine

1. Purposeful living is successful living.
2. It helps you realize your qualities and capabilities.

3. You escape a wasteful life.
4. You live your life to the fullest.

PRINCIPLE 10

Practice the Vision of Wholeness

You are the story of life being told. See your connection with the whole.

"Whatever is happening is part of the wonderful thing called Life."

Life is one organic whole and we are all parts of it. We are interrelated and interdependent. It is one story; your story is being told in all and through all of life. The victor's story includes all of the people and conditions he or she encountered. Similarly, Life's story is your story being told. When you make the story good for someone, you improve your own story.

We breathe out carbon dioxide; the plants breathe that in and breathe out the oxygen we need to breathe in for our survival. The house you live in or the roads you walk upon came into being through the agency of many types of artisans. The television set you watch was manufactured with components from many countries. Take a look around you and you will realize that very few indeed, or perhaps none, of the things you enjoy are produced by you. Some of the things you enjoy have traveled halfway around the world to you.

We are integrated in complex ways such that what affects one person in any part of the world affects everyone on the planet. Cruelty or injustice to one person is cruelty and injustice to the whole of life.

You must grow, therefore, the human selfishness into self-wholeness. Selfishness is the fishing for the self; it is the "I, Me, My, Mine, Myself" consciousness. When this consciousness grows, it becomes "I, Me, My family." It grows further into "I, Me, My tribe, "I, Me, My nation," and "I, Me, My race," etc. So you see that families, tribalism, nationalism, and patriotism are all various sizes or shades of selfishness. Selfishness is so subtle that people who preach nationalism and patriotism are not aware that they are advocating selfishness on a larger scale.

We, therefore, realize that the problem of man is not tribalism, or racialism, etc. The core problem of man is the inability to grow selfishness into self-wholeness. Peace and progress for mankind occurs when selfishness is transformed into self-wholeness.

Often, people talk about the ego or selfishness as something bad. They tend to see the ego as another part of themselves and all efforts are geared towards the overcoming of the ego. You cannot destroy the ego; it is an essential and natural part of you. What is natural cannot be destroyed. Selfishness is the power that gives you your sense of uniqueness. The ego is divine; you just have to work with it. The ego and its selfish nature are not evil.

Selfishness is natural and cannot be destroyed. It is what gives you a sense of identity. Having a sense of identity is a natural program of life. It is the reason we have a different thumbprint from that of anyone else. That is nature's way of celebrating diversity. To destroy selfishness is to destroy the psychic voice of your inner soul. The only problem is when you do not grow the ego and its selfish nature into self-wholeness. So, selfishness is not the problem; not growing it is the problem. You cannot grow what you do not have or have destroyed.

First, embrace selfishness and then grow it to self-wholeness. If your child does not grow or walk, you seek medical attention. Similarly, you need spiritual medicine for the growth of selfishness into self-wholeness.

Selfishness is to think and function from your finite sense of things. It is the state of being divorced, isolated from all others; seeking to be comfortable with yourself. Self-wholeness grows you to see how your uniqueness is interdependent on the uniqueness of all others and how you share the resources of life with all others. The air you just breathed in came from the nostrils of that friend or so-called enemy; you are standing on the earth that your friend or enemy is standing on; the same sun is touching you and you are all eating from the common bowl of the ocean or of Mother Earth. Stop being silly; you have no enemies. The person who eats with you from the same bowl cannot be an enemy. This awareness opens your eyes to see the cosmic purposes of your spouse, friends, and all people on the earth. Your actions, for example, cannot and must not stop or limit your spouse or anybody else in his or her cosmic dream or its execution. You know that stopping such a dream is stopping the creation of the new raw material or semi-processed materials you need for your own progress. This gives you a cosmic vision. You do not only see the cosmic activity in all; your presence demands it from all.

There is only one self – the spiritual self that is present as the self of all people and of all life. The fishing for the self ensures that all of its parts are served. To transform selfishness to self-wholeness requires that you identify the whole self and fish for it. It is as simple as that. Selfishness is fishing for the egoistic drive of the self; it is fishing for a perceived limited part of the self. Self-wholeness is fishing for the wholeness of the self. This whole self embraces the selves of all people.

Give passionate attention to your highest good in ways that inspire the highest good of all people. It is not necessary for you to get and give away; it is for you to get in such a way that in the process others are well served.

The vision of wholeness is to see the whole picture of life and not to see it only in bits and pieces. All things happen for a deeper reason than is apparent.

Life is friendly and generous and will not present disaster without warning. Many beasts and animals can sense natural disasters and move to safety before they occur. The sophistication of mankind and their dependency on the external instead of on the spirit numbs them to the voice of spirit. If you are caught in any disaster, however, gracefully surrender your body to the macro good of all life. Your life is secure and your spirit is safe. It is only your body that you surrender.

Whole Life Healing

Every thought, feeling, and action you initiate affect all on this planet and beyond, even rippling across time to affect generations yet to be born. This places a huge responsibility on you. However, as a divine being, you can handle the responsibility with ease. Watch for all thoughts and feelings that invade your mental field. Welcome them; they came to be filtered and purified, then to be released in order to circulate. An invading thought is like an idea from someone to you; it is in need of counseling. Welcome the thought and advise the thought. For example, when a thought of stealing comes to mind, arrest it and tell it that there is abundance. Now say mentally, "This thought of stealing returns to its source with the full knowing that there is abundance for all and that unlimited opportunities exist for us to be more of ourselves and to have more." Through this practice you cleanse the world.

We are dependent on one another. For your enjoyment, components from many countries come together for the manufacture of a television. The world is one garden of God with many flowers, music with many verses, and one human kingdom of God with many races, tribes and cultures. You need the presence of every atom in life; you need the presence of every person of every tribe, race, and creed in life.

The vision of wholeness frees you from seeing life in bits and pieces, a way of seeing that breeds pain. When in a movie theater you see the hero stabbed and concluding that the hero is dead you walk out of the movie early feeling bad, you have seen only a part of the movie. The movie may end up with the hero triumphant. Failing to see the whole picture of life breeds judgment and pain. To see the whole picture, you have to dialogue with life to know its intention for whatever is happening.

Selfishness makes you see what is happening only to you. Self-wholeness makes you realize that what is happening to you is happening to all of life. Though it may be painful for you, still there is good in it for all. Everyone contributes to the good of all. Natural disasters may be ways that life is balancing itself. They do not happen to some selected people; they happen for the good of all.

Storms at sea may wreck sailing boats; however, the storms are the ways that oxygen mixes with the water for the survival of fish. Many people depend on fish for food; fish need oxygen, and the storms at the sea provide that.

Volcanoes provide fertile soil. If you are caught up in storms or in a volcanic eruption, it may be the result of an error in your perception. You probably did not listen to life's warning.

Your life and your soul force are expanded by the number of people they bless. If your life is bringing peace to the whole, you become the center of concentrated peace and the whole energy of peace in the universe channels through you.

Whatever you go through, ask your inner self, "What is life seeking to do through this for the good of the whole universe?" Asking this question instantly spreads the challenge to the wholeness of life. You no more see an issue than you must deal with it. You see a world issue and the world supplies you with its huge solution, and this solution increases your capability to handle the issue in ways that bring good to all. You are no more handling personal issues; you are handling world issues and you do it responsibly. When you merge with life to solve a problem, the problem becomes small and insignificant. The vision of wholeness grows you into a universal being.

A person with universal consciousness sees shared challenges and resources. For example, a woman with universal consciousness will not see herself childless or inferior just because she is infertile. She does not see other women more favored than her. The whole of life has good reasons for her not having a child and it is okay. With universal consciousness, she will enjoy motherhood by enjoying the children of the world. The ability to have children is not a personal achievement; achievement lies in raising children or growing souls. She, therefore, sees herself as fertile because she sees the fertility of women demonstrated all around her. In any case, being infertile in childbearing does not stop her from being fertile in other areas.

Life blesses you from many points. To embrace wholeness is to be open to blessings from all angles. If you were to separate yourself from a group of people or to be prejudiced towards someone, you block the flow of blessing that may come from that connection. We are interrelated and interdependent in the wholeness of life. Every part is important in the wholeness.

How to Practice Wholeness

The practice of wholeness does not require you to surrender your uniqueness.

It requires you to focus on your uniqueness and to contemplate other people's uniqueness as well as how their uniqueness enhances what you are.

Similarly, notice how your uniqueness enhances and expands the uniqueness of others. This contemplation opens you to a conscious embrace of wholeness.

The sense of wholeness frees you from being overwhelmed by world events.

Practice One

What joyful, creative thoughts have passed through your mind today?

Release this thought to the world and let the world know its benefit. Make time to celebrate the wonderful thoughts that have celebrated you.

Bring in painful thoughts and dialogue with them. Embrace them and learn their reason for being there with you.

Transform them and release them to their source – that is, from the minds of the people who originated the thoughts.

Here is an example: when a thought of stealing comes to your mind, say this: "I love this thought of stealing. I bring to the awareness of this thought that many countries have abundant food and throw the excess away; they throw away food that is then eaten by birds and animals. Now I release you to go to your source with this awareness and with joyful blessings."

The thought will return to its source with this new awareness and that is your contribution to the whole self that includes you and the originator of the thought.

Practice Two

A magical practice that transforms every challenge into an asset is to look into the face of the challenge, embrace it, and address it by directly saying: "What is life seeking to do through this challenge (name it) for the good of the entire planet?"

This soul enquiry lifts that problem or difficulty from you to the world. It makes the problem a challenge of all mankind and the collective intelligence of all mankind provides you with solution. When you lift up the problem as a universal problem, universal solution flows in to solve it. Sometimes after this enquiry you may experience nothing in the moment. A day or two after, a person comes to you with the solution or the problem resolves itself. This works because you make the micro problem an issue for the macro to solve; you made the selfish problem a self-whole issue so you draw in vast spiritual energy to handle it. This is a miracle practice, so do it.

Practice Three

Notice your goodness.

Notice the ways your goodness is blessing and expanding those in your environment.

It is a daily, moment by moment practice of asking, "How is the good I am blessing and expanding the spiritual riches of this person I am talking to?"

This lifts your vision above pettiness and human weakness; it empowers you to be the divine and calls the same from all of life. You are a walking blessing. As you practice this attitude, life supplies you with the ability to expand the lives of all who share your life. No one goes away from you unblessed.

Dare to see the whole picture of life and you will realize that this world is paradise and that you are a wonderful contributor and a part of it. The universe is contained within you.

We all have a responsibility to make life sweet.

It is egoistic to think that you have to solve your own problem. In self-wholeness, you make it a universal problem and embrace the solutions of life. Life is like a mutual fund; you share the profit and losses. The battle is the Lord's and the Lord is revealed as the life of every person on the planet, so release your problem to the Lord.

Practice Four

Do all the good you do for your own highest good, remembering its connectedness with all. Be mightily served in the service you give to another. The practice of Self wholeness is to do things in ways that serve your highest selfish interest. When a man is aware of how the good he does for a family will help to grow sons and daughters who may marry his dear children, he would do it with passion.

Self Wholeness is the vision of how our cosmic interconnectedness serves our individual interests.

Lessons on the Principle of Wholeness

1. You represent all of life.

2. You cannot live in isolation; life is about your highest good.

3. We are dependent on one another and we share the same resources.

4. Your life must bring the highest good to all and to yourself.

Benefits of Principle Ten

1. You see life as one organic whole, hence you naturally honor all life forms.

2. You do not see life in bits and pieces; you see the whole picture of life and thus increase in knowledge, understanding, and wisdom.

3. You develop universal consciousness.

4. You are supportive of life.

5. You do not carry the burdens of life alone. You realize these burdens are not yours only. They are life's challenges and life has solutions.

PRINCIPLE 11
Something for God to Do

Free yourself from the burden of responsibility.

To feel responsible for someone is a superiority drive. To verify this, just close your eyes and say 'I am responsible for…,' and mention the person's name. you will feel and sense of superiority over the person, so you are on superiority drive.

Feeling responsible for someone leads to frustration, anxiety, and waste of life. Man is too complex for you to be responsible for. The forces that affect him are numerous, stemming from the infinite past to the infinite future. What happens to a person and why it happens have many remote causes. To know all of these causes is impossible; it is not meant to be that way. To feel responsible for someone is like feeling responsible for the amount of moonbeam that the moon is able to reflect at a given time. Sweet as the moonbeam is, it is impossible to hold it in your hands. Feeling responsible for someone cages you into the limitations of the person; it stifles you and blurs your vision of possibilities.

We are partners in life, never meant to be responsible for one another. We support each other to the degree that the spiritual resources life is given to us.

When life endows you with resources, it calls on you to use them to advance the wholeness of life. To stop yourself from using the resources you have to advance life is a violation of the law of use and, as recorded in the parable of the talents you will lose your resources if you don't use them. *"Unto him who has, more is given; but unto him who has not, even the little he has is taken away.*

You do not have responsibility for anyone's welfare except your own. When you are well, the world around you will be well. To the degree that you are responsible for yourself, you allow Spirit to be responsible to a larger field of souls through you and in that you are enlarged. To be responsible implies absolute care for someone or something and that is impossible. This does not mean you should not live a responsible life. Responsible living is to respond adequately to the call of your internal needs and to those of others. You are not, however, responsible for anyone. You may do your best for someone; however, his response or non-response depends on several factors, some predating this lifetime. A parent, for example, may do the best for his or her child, yet the child may become delinquent. The factors responsible for this development lie beyond the parents so they must not blame themselves for not being able to do better.

A typical example is when a woman is caught up in the blame for the death of her child. There is the feeling of 'if I had been there or done this or that, my child would not have died.' Nature is too vast to be contained by you. You cannot be responsible for the air that your child breathes, for the food that they eat and for the grounds they walk on or the water that they drink. Each of these could be careers of disease, germs and viruses etc.

Your responsibility is to be and remain healthy and to the degree of the strength you have, you would be able to care for many including your own. *You cannot be responsible for the knowledge you did not have to salvage the situation.* It is life's duty to give you that knowledge and if it has not given you, then you did the best with your limited knowledge. Do not punish yourself by feeling inadequate for what you did not have the knowledge to accomplish. You re not meant to be to accomplish all things. To feel responsible in such instances will rob you of the knowledge you have and stall your potentialities. In self-blame, your potential is stalled and you cannot do that to yourself. If you do not have the heavens of knowledge to salvage the situation, do not rob yourself of the earth of potentials you have.

The only way to help the poor is to be rich and the only way to help the sick is to be healthy. Depriving yourself to poverty and sickness makes you a liability on the poor and the sick. A popular saying states; 'had I known is always at last.' The truth is 'had I known' was never late. You know when you should know. Step into the moment and enjoy the magic called life.

Releasing yourself from responsibility makes you see what is needed and then you can respond spontaneously to what is needed in a given time and space. Thus, you become the hand of spirit, working to fulfill itself. What may seem to be evil today will, tomorrow, unfold to great good. Embrace the dawn of eternity and all-knowledge in now. However, celebrate the life that flows through your soul. Do not let a misplaced sense of responsibility stifle you and cause wasteful anxiety, disease, and degeneration.

Anxiety is a good thing; it is your response to it that is the problem. Anxiety is your call to manifest some inner potentialities. It requires one or all of five things:

That you get up to do, teach, or render a service and that you give direction or seek help.

You are just a conscious presence and a hand that life uses to fulfill itself for all. You can do just as much as life chooses to do through you. The secret is to know how much life has equipped you to do and just be available to do that. For example, there are many types and sizes of water taps for various uses. Even though the ones in your bathroom can be used to fill a fire truck's water tank, they are, however, an inadequate tool; hydrants connected to a high-pressure water source are required for such a need.

When you free yourself from the human sense of responsibility, you become available to see what life is doing through other units. On subatomic and spiritual levels we are connected. Seeing the huge capabilities life has made available through others creates those capacities in you. You thus increase in your capacity to do more for others.

Life is an orchestration of many intelligent forces within the being of God. Many instrumentalists including you play the music of life with the intelligent purposeful conductor, God, present in every unit of the players and the instruments. You are a unit within God. God is the intelligent purposeful happening in and as the instrumentalists and their instruments and you cannot be responsible for God.

You cannot do it all. You are challenged to discover your abilities and use them in the best ways possible. When you seem to find no solution to a problem, it is an indication that it is to be handled by another God-presence. Do not fight this. When your best cannot do it, then, IT IS SOMETHING FOR GOD TO DO. Realize this and surrender gracefully to some other unit of the God-presence to take over.

It is not something for your wife, husband, friends, or parents to do. It is something for God to do, so relax and trust the process. It is not being done by your kids, supervisors, or subordinates. It is being done by God through other units, so trust the process of life and relax. Your anxiety weakens you. If Life chooses to do something through your spouse, kids, or parents, so be it. It is for God to do.

For example, you cannot be responsible for the perfection of everyone in your family. You cannot blame yourself for their mistakes and failures. You cannot prevent them from dying, if it is time. You cannot stop yourself from dying, if it is time. Life will, as it has always done, take care of those you leave behind. Many have left their children orphaned; however, many orphans have risen to great nobility. More than half of the population of mankind are orphaned sometime in their lives. Life's duties are done like a relay race. You cannot run the whole race, nor feel responsible for the failure of your team if you run your part to the best of your ability. Know where and when your capabilities end and hand over the baton to life. Let life do the task through you and it will be done in big ways.

Solve the problems that are yours to handle and gracefully give up what is beyond your reach. Whatever joyful or painful situation you may find yourself in, realize that you are not the first and you will not be the last. Life will go on even if you over-exert yourself to death. And life will continue to take care of life when you have passed on. One thing is certain, you will move on; so make your living an exclamation of joy. A joyful life is a blessing unto life.

Do not attempt to do God's work for God. It is impossible to do. God is vast; you can allow God to do her work through you. You are not responsible for another's problem or issue. You are responsible for you. When you are perfect, all around you will be perfect. The world is served better when you are rich, prosperous, happy, creative, and resourceful. Taking responsibility for life is too much for you to handle; let God do that and do your part in the process. Know when it is your business and know when it is time to surrender the issue or challenge to the Infinite Consciousness. Carrying the burden of being responsible for everything weakens you and that is a disservice to life. You are responsible for no one's life – not for the life of your children, parents, friends, or associates. Be responsible for you and do what will unfold the highest good that you are here for. When the good that you are is freely expressed, it serves others and enriches their lives and your duty is done. You are responsible for the whole world only to the degree that Spirit is responsible through you for the whole world. When Life wants you to do it, it will give you the wisdom and abilities to do it easily.

In sickness, people sometimes spend themselves to poverty even when they know quite well that there is no medical cure for them. The doctors have reached the end of their knowledge, but it is not the end of Life's knowledge. In surrendering the problem to Spirit, you relax and in that state, you are open to the miracle. Miracles often happen when people give up to Spirit.

Problems existed long before you were born and they will continue to exist when you are dead and gone. While alive, therefore, there is no point in your carrying them. Gracefully handle what you can and move on.

Beyond all you seek to do, there is a cosmic movement going on. This movement affects our individual lives. What is happening in a remote galaxy, light years away, is affecting everything in the universe and affecting your individual life. You cannot know it all; it's too much trouble to attempt such. Seek help when you have to; it is not all meant to be known and done by you. Participate in the flow. You must know when to do and when to give it up. Giving up is not to sink into hopelessness. It is to surrender joyfully into the universal machinery to fulfill itself. You step back and watch, ready to celebrate the glorious outcome.

Surrender

To surrender is to yield consciously and willingly to a higher power and dream. When you consciously and willingly yield to something, you must embrace whatever happens. You will not question or complain; you will trust implicitly. There is risk in surrender unless you clearly know what you are surrendering to.

This surrendering we are to do is about surrendering to God. Surrendering to God seems to have risks as well. There are times when God does not seem to make sense. Here are a few examples.

1. A couple with their three children was returning from Church. Just before arriving at their house, they were swept down by a semi truck. The man and two of the children died. The widow and one child survived with several injuries. Who would this woman cry for? What vision would she see in another marriage or for the future at the age of 50? What would she think of God?

2. In early 2005, the Tsunami disaster occurred. Tidal waves as a result of a sea volcano swept through the land killing over two hundred thousand people.

3. In an earthquake in Iran, 50,000 people died.

4. You may have your personal stories of being cheated, raped, abused, rejected, etc.

Life seems insensitive when you think of these occurrences.

God is really saying:

"Just to have night and day, I am spinning the earth at 1000 mph for you. Do you know the weight I am spinning? It is 6×10^{27} metric tons. To give you seasons, I am also moving it through space at the same time at the speed of 67,000 mph, tilted on its axis. I must have a deep respect for you. I would not do these things if I did not care about you. I have set your heart to beat 40,000,000 times a year without your conscious input. Rise and surrender to your own higher life. When I have formed you for immortality, what is death? If death there be, then even the sun will one day die."

To surrender is to release the little vision of yourself into the great vision God has for you. Most pain is the result of your thinking you are mortal. The mortal sense sees death as a loss. In the spiritual sense, life is pure energy; thus, there is no loss.

Trust Life's Goodness

Life is good, I say, and life has outdone itself to provide for your good. The intelligent goodness of life provided you with blood, oxygen, and food when you were helpless in your mother's womb. It changed the chemistry of your mother to produce breast milk before you were born. Knowing that your fragile body may not be able to handle the harsh environment you suddenly find yourself it, life provided antibiotics in the colostrum, the first breast milk to sustain you. All you needed is provided before you needed it. That is the law and nature of life.

Even if your body is being eaten by worms, think of the great good happening for your sake, and be still. Give up; not unto hopelessness, but to Spirit to take over.

Lessons on the Principle of Responsibility

1. You are not meant to do it all. When your best is done, it is time to surrender to God.

2. Taking responsibility for life is burdensome and eventually makes you irresponsible to yourself. Do your part and let life do the rest.

3. You are responsible for the whole world to the degree that Spirit is responsible through you.

Benefits of Principle Eleven

1. You trust the self-supporting goodness of life.

2. You are available to be you and to enjoy being you.

3. You release the burden of responsibility unto Spirit.

4. You see the great good happening in life and this makes human challenges insignificant.

If the sun rises and does not set, life on earth will perish and if the darkness should rise and not set, life will equally perish. The intelligent purpose behind the rising light and darkness is, therefore, God. You take this process for granted, don't you? God starts as and from the intelligent purposeful happening in your mind, body, and feelings through all space you see and beyond. God, then, is the next person, plant or animal, earth or stars you see and beyond.

PRINCIPLE 12
The Practice of Love and Confidence

See the good and the divine or the possible good and the divine in all of life and in yourself.

Love is the most compelling force in life. It creates and changes people's lives and destinies. It builds people and nations and destroys them as well. It is the subject for over ninety-five percent of all music composed. It is the most flattering energy and the most abused as well. This dichotomy of love makes it a dilemma and a frustration of life. We need a workable definition of love that would make its presence and practice a joyful one.

Love is the driving force of the universe. The word *love* is used and abused more than any other word. People love to love, speak about it, compose songs about it, decorate it, and desecrate it. Its energy produces happiness and sorrow. When you know what love is, then its sacredness will be preserved and it will be the ever-healing force that it is meant to be. Just what is love?

Love is not a sentiment; it is a discipline. In my fervent search on how to practice love, I discovered this definition for love: "Seeing the good and the divine or the possible good and the divine in all of life and in yourself." What is good, beautiful, and divine excites your affection and adoration and, of course, your love. You can, therefore, not love yourself or another unless you see the good in yourself and in the other person. If you can see the good that the enemy is or see the possible good that the enemy could be, the history of the pain that caused the enmity will be healed and you will begin to love him or her.

There is a deep cry in all people to be seen and known for what they really are. Often we confuse what a person is with what a person does and we confuse what we are with what we do. When you have a friend who practices medicine, you are likely to see him always as a doctor. You may even forget that this person has feelings and thoughts like any ordinary person. This forgetting may develop to the extent that you lose touch with what he or she really is as a person.

What you do is the coat you put on. What you do includes the things you have learned from your culture for survival. You have attitudes that protect you; other attitudes are to help you face the world or to get your way. These are all things you do but they are not what you are.

You are confident when you believe that you are truly seen without the masks of attitudes. When you have any reason to feel that your true self cannot be seen and your attitudes cannot shield you, you lose confidence. One of the major causes for loss of confidence is the fear of rejection. You want to fit into the boxes of people's opinions for fear that you will be rejected if you don't. Interestingly, people's opinions are dependent on other people's opinions. This means that people do not, in fact, have their own opinions.

To seek to fit into boxes of people's opinions is to become an amoeba, a shapeless ever-changing creature; you will be following a mirage. You end up stopping your own true self from its free expression. You thus deny life your true presence and beauty. Such a wasted life does not befit you.

Often you do not see the good and the divine in yourself because you focus on what you do instead of what you are. Your actions make you feel unworthy. Beyond what you do, there is a fine, sacred you that lies within. It may not be outwardly evident; all the same, when you find this you inside of yourself, you find something about you that is pure. To make contact with that you is the first step of self love.

When you do something stupid and someone calls you a stupid person, you feel hurt. This is because a sacred part of you says, "I have done something stupid but that does not make me a stupid person." What you did was stupid, but that is only what you did. It is not what you are.

People label you by what you do. They scarcely see what you are. To accept the labels people put on you can lead to self-negation. Even if the labels are positive ones, they can influence you to ignore the vital sacred you.

To awaken to what you are, practice constant introspection with these prompts: "What do I know about myself that is not dependent on what my parents or others have told me?" "What do I know about myself that no one knows and how do I live the life of the person I know that I am?"

With the discovery of the real you, you will come to the discovery of your inner potential. There is only one of you and it cannot be repeated. Nothing in your past or your expectations for the future can describe you. You are a field of infinite potential, and you deserve to celebrate yourself. When you do, then life will celebrate you.

The good you see in the world is the good you really are. What you do not have you cannot give. If you do not have love for yourself, you cannot love anyone else. If you see life as good and abundant, that is what you really are.

Self-love is very difficult without an appreciation of the outer world. When you can see the goodness of life as the air you breathe, as the sunshine, and as the water you drink to nourish your body, you begin to appreciate what a precious and valuable person you are for life to have contrived to serve your needs in such abundant and precise ways. Practice loving your world and you will constantly discover your own magnificence.

Love is the driving force of the universe and the energy that propels each person to be the light and to be the best they can be. Many have stalled this essential force because of some experience which they have misinterpreted. An experience of pain either self-caused or unleashed on you by others leads you to the negative description of yourself as unworthy, inadequate, downtrodden, or unacceptable, and these descriptions create corresponding energies within you which stall your growth and progress. You, therefore, find it difficult to love yourself.

Your confidence similarly is eroded. When you see energies seeming to work against the good you are at the core of your being, you lose confidence and you do not love yourself and have no drive to be. These negatives are very strong forces and you need to uproot them in order to appreciate yourself and thus be confident. Confidence is nothing but standing tall in the goodness that you are or can be. Consider how you describe yourself by your experiences:

If you experience loss, are you are a loser?

If you experience rejection, are you unworthy?

If you experience lack, are you poor?

Be conscious of the difference between an experience you have and your core values, and you will maintain your self-love and confidence. Fuel your energy by loving and honoring the real you. When you come to your real self, you realize that you do not describe yourself by what you do and experience rather than by what you are. Your experiences are not you, nor can they describe what you are. You are something sacred that is more than all of your past experiences together. You are the energy and power that causes and receives the experience; therefore, you cannot be the experience.

Bring to mind some of the nice experiences you have initiated and look for the wonderful person inside of you that initiated them and you will be in touch with the love in you.

Realize this: your body is for you to use for this lifetime. One day, in death, you will no more be able to use it. Why keep your body silent in life when it will be silent in death? Speak out when you must and be freely expressive. Only you can do it the way you do it. If what you do is wrong, make a correction. No one is perfect. Making mistakes is the way of growth.

Whatever you do may either be approved of or disapproved of by others and that is normal. Do not stop doing what you are capable of doing because of someone else's opinion. Nature approves of itself. It rains when it must, volcanoes erupt when they must, the sun shines as it should; all these natural events occur without your approval. Nature approves of itself and so must you. Ask for help when you need it. It is no shame to know less than others. In some other area you know more that they know. There are three answers when you ask for help and they are: "Yes," "No," and "Wait." Prepare for any of these answers; use any help you do receive and move forward. None of these answers is meant to shame you and even if they were, you have exercised your right to ask. Many have said no to a request for help and regretted it later. Even if the whole world says no to your highest dream, go ahead and do it, knowing that you and God form a majority. Love yourself so much that you are ready to stand up for what you believe in. Do not choke yourself to death on the opinions of others.

The absence of confidence is the absence of love. Love is often said to start with one's self. Unfortunately, this does not work. We are so externally focused that we do not see ourselves. A useful practice is to love the world first and then realize that you are an integral part of it.

Watch for the beauty in the orderliness, precision, and spontaneity of life. Identify similar harmony in your mind, feelings, and body, and you will be held spellbound by the "awesome you" that must be loved. Watch the perfect functioning of your organs alone and you will embrace yourself in perfect love. The ratio between good and seeming evil is that of the ocean and a drop of water. The universe is happening: it is moving, yet stable; that is beauty at its best.

By seeing the good or the possible good, you lift your consciousness to the state of being the manifestation of divine goodness.

How to Practice Love

Like any discipline, love must be practiced in order to be mastered. The master Jesus summed up the whole of spiritual law as love. He taught, "Love God with all your heart and might and your neighbor as yourself." If you do not love yourself, you will not be conscious of the love that is reaching you from dear ones around you and from life, nor will you be able to love God. Love should start with self-love; however, self-love is rather difficult for the majority, so love the world and see how the vastness of life serves the wonderful and deserving you.

1. Identify and list all the good that you appreciate life for. Give conscious attention to what you see life doing for you.

2. Identify and list all that you love and appreciate yourself for.

3. Identify and list all the good and divine things you have ever done for someone or for life, such as the kindness, care, or support you showed or gave to someone.

Identify and list all your achievements, great and small, such as your ability to wash your hands, clean your clothes, and pass your exams.

Read these lists to yourself and contemplate how the universe supported you by giving you knowledge to achieve these things. You will be absorbed in love for yourself, for your neighbor, and for the intelligent force of the universe.

To help you to love your neighbor more dearly, list all of the good or possible good which that person has done for you or for any other unit of life. No matter what the depth of pain this person may have caused you, reading this list will reduce the pain and absorb you in love and respect for him or her.

A Loving Way of Life

Let this be your state of living:

I am very busy admiring, celebrating and watching what God is doing with my life.

I did not create myself; let the Creator take care of his creation that I am.

In practice, "Love is seeing the good and the divine or the possible good and the divine in all of life and in yourself." This practice enlarges your vision. You begin to see the ideal world that God is unfolding. You are not trapped in little occurrences; you are a cosmic observer of the good that is unfolding and you naturally attract that good into your experience.

Lessons on the Principle of Love and Confidence

1. Accept yourself. Only you can do it the way you do it.

2. It is no shame to know less about a subject; and you are not less for knowing less. Ask for help when you need it.

3. Love starts with self-love. You cannot love another if you do not love yourself.

Benefits of Principle Twelve

1. You experience healing and growth.

2. You increase in confidence and peace.

3. Your creativity is enlarged.

4. You are perpetually joyful.

PRINCIPLE 13
The Power of Choice

Choose consciously.

Life created us to have free will; free will gives us the power of choice. Life is a field of infinite choices that come together to give birth to new products, which life in turn endows with the power to make choices. You are, therefore, presented with an infinite variety of choices and this may be overwhelming.

Each moment, you are making choices – choices in thoughts, feelings, and actions. Most often, however, you do not make your choices; you allow choices to make you. When you go to a shop to buy something and you see any varieties of the thing you want, do you choose what you want or do you allow the product to choose you? You choose your experiences. So, choose the thoughts, feelings, and actions that celebrate you.

The combination of choices you make determines your happiness or sorrow, your success or failure, your creativity or destructiveness, your invincibility or vulnerability, your truthfulness or falsehood, your Godhood or human-hood.

Unlike animals we have the capability to choose independently of the circumstances in which we find ourselves. Animals are influenced by Time, Energy, Space, and Circumstance. Animals may hide in their holes during winter while humans can choose to carry on with their lives. Man is not ruled by the condition he lives in; he has the power of choice and the inner power to act on it. Inappropriate use of choice brings pain and the reverse is true.

If you have ever gone shopping and regretted your purchase when you arrived home, it is an indication that the product chose you or that you made an unconscious choice. To heal this phenomenon, scan through your mind to identify the elements that caused you to make the unconscious choices. Consider things like advertising, trends, and other people's opinions. Whatever led you into an unconscious choice loses its power when you become conscious of it.

Expectation, Opinion, and Interpretation

The greater part of your life is managed by the powers of Expectation, Opinion, and Interpretation. These are your angels or devils depending on the choices you make.

When your expectations are based on the past and on the expectations of your parents, friends, or partners, you are lost. You are trying to live other people's expectation. Investigate your expectations to find out whose expectations you have. Sometimes your expectations are based on what you think people are expecting or will be expecting. Meanwhile, you do not even know who the people are who would have those expectations. You are being ruled by a large unconscious field of expectation. You may have heard people make generalized statements like "Everyone thinks this or that." When you ask who specifically thinks that way, the person may not be able to name more than two people, and most of the time, none. It was only what that person thought people would think. Such is the unconscious living of a lost soul.

By all means, have great expectations for yourself, for your every moment, and for your future. Expect the highest and the best for your life. With eagerness, embrace God's intention for you and expect it to happen.

Take care, however, that your expectations do not bring you anxiety, tension, or stress. Others have rights to their own expectations. If you allow your expectations to be imposed upon others, you open yourself to disappointment and pain. When you place your hope and expectations on others, you create in your soul room for disappointment. Let not the highest and the best you expect of others outstrip the highest and the best you are in yourself in the moment.

You have a choice in what to expect and in how to expect it.

Like expectations, opinions are based on history. Opinions can support or destroy you. People's opinions are changing constantly. To fit into people's opinions is to become a shapeless creature. You have to make your choice. If people fail, they often blame those whose opinion they have followed. If things go well, they praise themselves. Make your choice out of life's numerous opinions and take responsibility for the outcome. Once you use an opinion, it ceases to be someone else's opinion; it is now yours.

How could the world grow without opinions? Opinion brings the minds of the bright and the dull together where they create the various shades for the picture to be formed.

Everyone is entitled to his or her opinion and so are yours to you. Your opinions and those of others you choose to accept are entirely yours. You can choose to be injured by your own opinions or those of others. You can also choose to be prospered by opinions. Opinions are the gifts of ideas to you and only you can choose what to do with them. You can embrace them, use them, reject them, or ignore them. Opinions are rarely independent and most people's opinions are dependent on those of others.

You have a choice as to what opinions, out of millions available to you, you open yourself to and how you use them. If you choose to respond to all opinions or be vulnerable to them, you will end up losing your sense of identity and you will be confused and miserable.

From colors to sounds and ideas, you are always interpreting. Interpretation is your power to relate with the world around you. Through interpretation, you enter into your invisible world of ideas and process whatever you are going through. Interpretation determines your response to what is happening around you. Through interpretation, you create the laws that rule your life.

Two people cannot give the same interpretation of a simple flower or picture. There are infinite interpretations to whatever is happening in your life. You have the power and choice to vary the interpretation you put to an event and thus make it feel good or bad.

Watch your interpretations; they may be coming from past conditioning. Are you seeing with your eyes or with the colored spectacles of yesterday? If yesterday's spectacles are clouded, make them clear. Many people do not even see with their own eyes; they choose to see through the eyes of others and thus lose touch with their inner values.

You have a choice in your thoughts, feelings, and actions. To every event there are millions of joyful as well as sad interpretations you may give to it. You have a choice of what interpretations to select from your infinite storehouse. Choose thoughts, feelings, expectations, and interpretations that celebrate you. Everyone else may see a bad situation, but you can choose an interpretation that brings you joy – the choice is always yours. Medicine has saved millions of lives. If it fails, society condemns it as though it were practiced by demons. They give it all sorts of painful interpretations. You have a choice in this; be conscious of your choice. Good outnumbers error to a ratio of a zillion to one. To every event, give an interpretation that honor you and bring you joy.

Choosing your Thoughts

The mastery of choice is the mastery of life. Imagine that you can choose your thoughts and feelings. Then you can take calculated, premeditated actions with predetermined results that make you a God in your world and that is what you are.

Scan through your life and see how thoughts, feelings and actions have been more or less imposed on you from the environment. With the mastery of choice, you can choose your heaven here and now. Life presents you with an overwhelming amount of variety for your use. If you do not master choice, you are overwhelmed and the varieties in life use you instead of your using them; thus, you become an effect of the environment instead of being the cause of it.

You are drowned in an ocean of seeming conflicting thoughts, and feelings, desires, expectations, opinions, and interpretations. You are not living life, and then suddenly there comes death and you are gone. One lifetime wasted; an eternal semester lost. To live under the weight of unconscious choices is sleepwalking. You can wake up and you will.

Reaction

You are always teased by the events in life to react. It's okay to react; the question is, what are you reacting to? Reaction is to re-act to what is done to you or brought to your attention.

When you react, therefore, you are doing the same thing that you have seen the other person do.

Often reactions are to some wrongdoing. Most of the times in reacting you want to act out with greater force. When what you are reacting to is someone's wrongdoing or stupidity, you end up doing more wrong or acting stupid yourself.

Similarly, when you react to a loving situation you have experienced, you feel more loving. It is important to remind yourself whenever you are about to react to something that your reaction is going to either reduce or increase you. It reduces when the reaction is to error and increases when it is for good.

Everyone, including the ignorant and stupid, knows how to react; it takes the wise to react otherwise. There is nothing special to reaction and it gives you no sense of achievement.

Choose to act consciously, with an awareness of the positive results from your actions. What is done to you affects one primary person and that is you. Always be in the state of mind that asks, "What action of mine can bring a joyful result to me and to all concerned?" Asking this question will make you watch over your reaction.

Even if your reaction is to something loving, you may end up loving foolishly. Act consciously and act in your own way, in a way that brings you greater joy.

Reaction may give you a temporary sense of satisfaction. However, in the deepest parts of you, you may contact places of depression, regret, and remorse as a result of the reaction.

When the wise and the ignorant argue, to the onlooker both are stupid. In every situation you may probe into yourself, "What action is being called forth to bring out the highest good?"

Reaction is your unconscious response to external stimuli. Action is the conscious move to do what you consider needed to be done. Choose to act and act consciously, knowing its repercussions.

Be Abnormal

What is normal must not grieve the soul. It is normal for people to blame their failures and inadequacies on you. The normal reaction of most people to this blame is to fight back or eat their hearts out with sorrow. Choose to be different; choose to be 'abnormal.'

To divert attention from their weaknesses, people always point accusing fingers at others. Every ill of which you accuse someone might be something you have done before or are still doing. A person who accuses constantly is advertising his or her own weaknesses. The normal reaction is to defend, and defense is an attack. A better way of handling such people is to be abnormal. Instead of wasting your strength in fighting back, show the accuser his or her strength.

Think of other abnormal attitudes of strength you can choose to use. By all means, if an accuser takes you to court, hire an attorney to defend you. However, focus on what strength in the accuser is seeking expression and support it. This practice lifts you above ordinary thinking and makes you a universally acceptable person.

Practice One

Make the following statements several times and pause in between to ask yourself, "What is God's idea about me?" When you have a clear picture of God's idea about you, choose to be it instantly.

- I am a divine idea of God whose time has come.

When you are sufficiently done, make the next statement several times. Pause in between and identify what is unlike God.

- God, purify me of anything unlike you.

Practice Two

1. Allow your eyes to close.

2. Be still and notice the thoughts and feelings that come into your mind. Entertain both the desirable and undesirable ones.

3. Now make the statement, "Loving thoughts are here." Smell, taste, listen to, feel, and see what loving thoughts are like. To do this, probe into yourself, saying, "If loving thoughts have smell, what is the smell like?" Do the same for the other senses.

4. Change your quest to peaceful thoughts, joyful thoughts, etc. Allow your eyes to open when you are done.

Practice of Conscious Choice

You are consciousness and, thus, are a conscious being. The art of life is to make conscious choices always. Over the years, you may have succumbed to external influences and lost your ability to choose. With the following practices, you will recover it.

Practice Three

1. Present yourself with ideas, such as fruit or cars.

2. When the idea is fruit, for example, make your conscious choice on the type of fruit you want to think about. Be clear about the thoughts you want to think about the particular fruit and think them through. Smell, taste, feel, hear, and see the color of your chosen thought and notice the changes in smell, tastes, feel, sound, and color as you think the thoughts you have chosen to think about that particular object. Make it a daily game.

It may go like this:

"I present to myself the ideas of fruit."

"I choose to think about fruit." Consciously, bring your attention to fruit. "I choose to think about a mango. I am thinking that it has a taste of sweetness on my tongue. Its color is orange and green and its smell is sweet and I am bringing a joyous feeling to it … etc."

Next, you may choose another object for the exercise.

Practice Four

1. Have an object in mind.

2. Choose to think happy or sad thoughts about the object and think them. Or choose to have happy or sad feelings about the object and have them.

3. Choose to have happy thoughts and sad feelings at the same time about the object. This practice gives you mastery over thoughts and feelings.

With time, you will be so clear in consciousness that you can create an electronic antenna between you and the Cosmic Intelligence and downloads specific information to yourself. When your mind can choose a thought to think without distraction, you are truly conscious and yours is the mystical experience.

The whole point of this game is to be conscious of what you are choosing, moment by moment, and to be sure it is your choice; then life is fun.

Practice Five

In your daily routine, take a look at a green field and choose to think of a particular leaf. Look at your bookcase and choose to think about one of the books there. Observe your living room and choose to think about a particular piece of furniture. Listen to music and choose to hear one of the instruments playing it. Choose without internal or external compulsion.

Lessons on the Principle of the Power of Choice:

1. Each moment, you are making choices – choices in thoughts, feelings, and actions.

2. You choose your experiences.

3. Be conscious of the forces of Expectation, Opinion, and Interpretation. They can be both your angels and devils.

Benefits of Principle Thirteen

1. You choose consciously.

2. You make wise decisions.

3. You choose thoughts, feelings, interpretations, and expectations that bring you joy and are for your highest good.

PRINCIPLE 14

Mastery of the Senses

Liberate yourself from the servitude of the senses and rule life through them.

Almost all of the problems and woes of humans are due to their dependence on information received through the senses.

You are a spirit being living in an energy field of integrated intelligences. Your senses are intelligent beings. Through them you communicate with the outside world, both receiving and giving communication. Untrained, the senses have the capacity to choose how they present information to you. They make their own compelling demands on you and may dictate what your responses to the outside world should be. In short, it is what you hear and how you hear it; what you see and how you see it; what you taste and how you taste it; what you smell and how you smell it; and what you feel and how you feel it that influences your interpretations, conclusions, and subsequent actions.

You are not meant to be motivated either by your sense perceptions or by external influences. When you are fed by your senses instead of by your spirit, you are a prisoner and you live in confusion and pain. Pain, in this instance, embodies emotional, mental, and physical pain.

The goal of every person in life is self-liberation. Self-liberation is the liberation of the spiritual will from the servitude of the senses. The greatest part of you is lost through identification with the senses. Listen to your life and you will realize that you are always influenced by what you see, taste, hear, touch, and smell as well as by the thoughts of other people transmitted to you through your senses.

An example of this is, 'how does watching the news make you feel?' What emotions are triggered when you smell a rose? How about when you taste your Mum's cooking? Here is another illustration: take a mouth full of the tastiest food you like. Chew it and enjoy the taste and flavor but just before you swallow it, spit it out, take a good look at it and eat it again. I know you may be shuddering at the thought, because, as soon as you spit it out the spirit of sight sees it and says, 'you cannot have it' and succeeds in stopping you. This illustrates how much you are ruled by the senses. The senses are individual entities and they agree and disagree with themselves on issues. You must be conscious of how they operate so that you can exercise your direction over them, else, they are the boss in your life.

How to Be Conscious Through Your Senses

The conscious being enacts his will through the senses not vice versa. To the degree that you are led or motivated by your senses, you are unconscious. Those who live and enjoy only what the senses bring to them are the living dead; they are sleepwalking. The man who functions from the senses cannot experience and embrace God. Truly conscious beings invite the senses to celebrate what they are. Choose to be conscious and celebrate your life.

You were born free and though you are not in chains, you are fettered within your soul. You are not free to be you. You must dare to face the demons of your soul. You created them and thus they are your subjects. Face your dark side and reason out your weaknesses.

The way forward is to make friends with your senses. You cannot rule through them if you do not know them. A useful way to be conscious of your senses is to bring your attention to the sense of smell and choose to smell. Choose what you want to experience through your sense of smell. While eating for example, you may choose to smell only the onions. A practice my disciples do is to have two or more different fragrances. All are open before them, and they choose to smell just one of them. Do the same for the other senses. With hearing, choose only to hear the sound of the bass guitar in the music that is playing. Soon you will be able to act through the senses instead of their leading you and choosing your experiences for you. When you are able to instruct the senses in this manner, you are a conscious, living person. Knowing this and practicing this is mystical living.

Another practice is to notice a thought and observe what sense is generating that thought. Before you act on an emotion, ask your body to tell you which sense is responsible for the feeling or thought that produced it. You can ask, "What sense is bringing me this feeling or thought?" Then ask the other senses if they are in agreement before you follow the suggestion of the sense that brought in the thought. For example, the sense of smell may bring in a thought or feeling. When you ask the sense of hearing, it may disagree with that thought or feeling. Just dialogue with the senses and you will discover the mystery that you are.

The Bible says that flesh and blood cannot enter into the kingdom of God, meaning that the man who functions from the senses cannot experience and embrace God.

The senses have corresponding macro sensory systems in the world. A macro sensory system is the collective energy of a particular sense. Thus, we have a collective smell energy that is made up of the intelligence of the spirit of smell of all humans. Having dominion through the senses empowers you to have dominion over the macro sense systems, which run through all of mankind.

When you have gained mastery through the senses, then you can instruct them to specific tasks. You can take your stand in the center of the senses and order one sense to perform a task. You may pray saying, "Spirit of my hearing, connect yourself to the hall of knowledge and bring me information on how to bring about world peace."

Blessing the Senses

A mystical practice is to bless the senses. By blessing your senses, you become conscious of them and they in turn are conscious of your spiritual presence and supreme authority. They are aware of your voice and realize your spiritual presence that animates them. You are the light that lightens everything that comes into the world; you brought your senses into the world and you must ignite them with your light.

You are not of the world; therefore, you must lighten up the senses and they must obediently respond to you – their supreme God. It then becomes possible to instruct the senses what they must bring to you or take out. For example, you can instruct the sense of sight in the morning by saying,

"Spirit of my sight, minister to me by bringing unto me materials that will give me great joy."

You may instruct the sense of hearing saying, *"Spirit of my ears, bring me messages that will lift my spirit and make me rise to the citadel of divine glory."* Or, *"Spirit of my hearing connect to the hall of universal knowledge and bring me information on how to bring about world peace."*

It is only when you are able to instruct your senses in this manner that you can claim to be a conscious, living person; otherwise, you are dead. Having the senses and not being alive through them is to be dead. Knowing this and practicing it is mystical living.

Furthermore, you can stand in the mist of the senses and say, *"I in the midst of my sight, hearing, taste, smell, and touch, speak my word,"* and then you pray your word from a holistic you. Often, when you are praying, you may realize that some parts of you say no to your request. This means that there is no agreement between the senses. "When two or more agree in my name" refers not only to people but also to the senses, which need to be in agreement with a divine idea. A person may try to pray but if his senses are battling with him because of issues in his life, that person's spirit is considered dead. "When two or more agree in my name" also refers to two whole people and not two fragmented, broken down people. When people meet who are alive in and through their senses and are ruling the world through their senses, they create a unified force-field and their words are words of power.

If you do not practice blessing the senses and relating positively in and through them, you don't get a unified field but a scattered field. Hence the secret of a deep mystical living is to be awakened through the senses.

Lessons on the Principle of Mastering the Senses

1. Almost all of the problems and woes of human are due to dependence on information received through the senses.

2. Your senses are intelligent beings.

3. Conscious, living being enact their will through the senses and not vice versa.

4. Learn to know and be friends with your senses. In so doing you can exercise your will through them.

Benefits of Principle Fourteen

1. You are in true dominion because you rule through the senses.

2. When you are consciously free from the dictates of the senses you are truly free.

3. When you are conscious you cannot be manipulated.

PRINCIPLE 15
Accepting Life

This is the life you bargained for. Celebrate it as it is.

We live in an abundant, benevolent, and generous universe. That is not what most people see or experience. Most people see life as a problem to be solved; they never arrive at a solution and have to exit life. The greatest problem most people have is that they do not know what their real problem is. They find something about everything to complain about. Life is a perpetual grief to them.

To live in a pool of perpetual happiness, consider that you wake up one morning to discover that you have everything you have ever prayed for. You have a fleet of ultra modern self-driving cars and aircrafts; and you are dwelling in the most exquisite house that your imagination could conceive of. The streets are laid with silver and your drinking cups are of pure gold. You have food in infinite variety to last you a million centuries and at the press of a button or the transmission of a thought you are served. You have all things except that you are alone on the planet. How would that feel? Certainly it would be miserably boring. Man, naturally, wants to live with other people.

Often you lament why people are not as kind, understanding, good natured, and possibly perfect just as you are. Now suppose you woke up one morning, like in the previous analysis, to realize that all people on the planet are just like you in physical features, thinking, feelings, and actions. You have the same thoughts and act the same way at the same time, such that when you raise your hand all other hands are raised simultaneously; when you cry or laugh all others cry and laugh, etc. How would that feel? Like the previous one, it would be miserably boring because there would be, in effect, one person walking the whole world. Man wants to live with people who are different.

Therefore, find inner satisfaction with life because this is the world you have chosen. It is the world you always wanted. You would not like it otherwise. You have always wanted it with its variety of thoughts, feelings, and actions from other people.

Accepting Death

Now let us look at other causes of anxiety that produce a diseased mind, feelings, and body. This is the phenomenon called death. Most people are frightened at the mention of the name of this phenomenon, especially when it strikes those close to them. Once again, let us consider that you wake up in the morning to greet the sun and the sun decides never to set so it is daylight for all times. How would you like that? Again, it would be miserably boring. If day and night must be accepted as natural things to happen, so also must life and the transition called death be accepted. In truth, you are dying every split moment of a second and a new you is constantly being born. In about a year, you replace almost all of the cells that constitute the tissue of your physical body. If new suns and galaxies are being born, then, old ones will eventually die, including our sun. What is natural must not grieve. And if death were an end, then the setting sun would not rise again. This is life; we rise to a state of consciousness while at the same time we set (die) to another state of consciousness. The rhythm of the seasons, of the water cycle and of all life speaks of the rhythm of your life.

Observe your own spiritual bio-rhythm and enjoy the wonderment of your life.

Embrace Variety

From these three analogies flows the awareness that change and variety are the very things we chose before creation.

This is the world you have chosen. It is operating the way you wanted it to operate. People must necessarily be different; some short, others tall, some dark, and others fair. There must be varieties in character, nature, and attitudes. Most films you enjoy are the drama between the villain and the hero. The excitement of the film is determined by the sharp changes and variety of action that the film depicts. So this is the life you bargained for. You do not want it otherwise.

Find inner satisfaction with life. The ideal is to see, admire, and enjoy the expression of the One in its many forms. God has become everything for your complete happiness. God has become infinite varieties for your satisfaction. Look around at life and see the excitement in variety.

The healing key here is to move through life with adventurous excitement and passion. If necessary, exaggerate your passion for life until it becomes your reality. Imagine that you feel a creative passion for life; amplify and exaggerate this passion until it solidifies as reality. All of the technologies we see once existed only in the realms of the imagination, fueled by passion. Start each day by describing what a wonder it is. Exclaim how beautiful the plants are, and mean it.

You cannot live alone. The misunderstanding, misrepresentations, or whatever you may call them are all part of the wonderful 'thing' we call life. You are a life artist; you are to blend all shades of positive and negative emotions into a beautiful picture. Life does not care what happens to you. Life cares about what picture or music you make with what happens to you.

This is the world you have chosen. It cannot be otherwise, so love it.

Life without Standards

You must live a life without following other people's standards. You are the standard to yourself and hence you cannot expect people to be like you. Each person is unique and is on his or her authentic journey. You cannot expect people to change in order to be like you. The desire to change people to be like you comes from the need to have them relate well with you. To have harmonious relationships, change yourself to be in harmony with all others. Moment by moment, we are evolving. It is your calling to support others in evolving to their next stage in life. Helping others to unfold to their next stage automatically accelerates your own evolution. However, your evolution is slowed down when you want people to be like you, because you end up waiting for them to meet your expectations. You wait for them rather than moving forward with your own evolution.

It is your calling to evolve to your next stage. To evolve does not mean to meet the standards of other people. You are your own standard. Comparing yourself with others usually creates pain and distracts you from your own authentic course of evolution. Seeking to evolve to meet others' standards may create loss of identity, self-negation, and discontentment. You cannot be like someone else and you cannot make other people be like you. Celebrate variety; you are in yourself a field of variety. It is an exercise in futility to try to make people be like you or vice versa.

Be Available for Truth

Truth, it is said, is the cry of all but the game of few. Have you ever yearned for someone who has offended you to come out with the truth and then felt bad when that person did not speak the truth?

Truth is not only hard for many to speak; it is equally hard for many to hear. You cannot hear or know the truth until you are available for it. You are not available for truth yet you want others to be truthful.

Here is an example and it is not an isolated case. A lady came to me in great pain over her husband's infidelity. She traveled out of the country. On her return she was reliably informed by her husband's workers and relatives of her husband's infidelity. She does not usually read her husband's text messages on his mobile phone but prompted by pain, she read them and found a lot that confirmed what she was told. As would be expected her husband denied having had any dealing with any woman.

This woman was in pain; she felt betrayed, cheated, and unloved. "If only he would come out with the truth and confess," she sobbed sadly and bitterly. "He has cheated on me; and not only with one woman but with several while I was away," she concluded.

I helped her to analyze her pain in a session. First, is she prepared for the truth? Would she have been happy if the husband had told her to her face, "Yes, I went out with Doris and Mabel and they were fantastic"? Certainly, she would have felt disrespected. Was it possible that his lying was his way of saying that I have done wrong but I love and respect you? She believes that men should not cheat but is that the reality in life?

You are not being truthful if you do not face reality. You are not hurt by what people do; you are often hurt by the thoughts you have about what people do. You are not made weak by what people do; you are weakened by the thoughts you have about what people do. If your expectations do not embrace reality, you are living in pretense and lies. What is true and natural must not grieve you. Appreciate the weaknesses in people and the reasons for their weaknesses. Doing so will free you from pain and open you to enjoy life. A truthful life knows and accepts what is.

Lessons on the Principle of Accepting Life

1. Infinite variety is the nature of life and that is exactly what you bargained for. Yours is to enjoy the variety that is unfolding.

2. You do not need to have all people be like you.

3. Death is the other side of the coin of life.

Benefits of Principle Fifteen

1. You move through life with adventurous excitement and passion.

2. You are free from worry and anxiety.

3. You are uninfluenced by the attitudes of people.

PRINCIPLE 16
The Quest for Happiness

Place yourself at the Center of Happiness.

Happiness is looking at all the good and bad things in life and choosing to focus on the good things. Good is the natural state of life and happiness should come naturally to all. However, because you have identified with pain over a long period, happiness does not happen automatically. You must plan for happiness; if you do not, you are open to circumstances, expecting things to happen to make you happy. If your happiness depends on external forces, you reduce yourself to a beggar. You have the right to decide how much happiness you want to experience in a given day. When you begin to exercise this right, your consciousness opens to many things that are seeking to make you happy. Whatever makes you happy has power over you. It is, therefore, you who must choose what makes you happy and be available to it. In so doing, you are a master of happiness and you can determine to be happy in the midst of confusion.

Decide on the percentage of happiness you are to experience in a day and ask yourself, *"What do I need to do to be this happy?"* In so doing, the power of happiness is yours and you are not dependent on external factors to make you happy.

Often people think that life owes them happiness; so if they do not experience it, they find something to blame. They believe the power to be happy lies outside them. Decide to cause happiness to yourself and do it regularly. When you cause your own happiness you can have it always, because it is not dependent on external causes. Ask yourself, *"What can I cause in my spouse or boss to make me happy?"* In response, you will know what thought or action to initiate to make you happy. With such a practice, you are the master of your happiness.

Return to Center Of Happiness

We are going to consider two divine enquiries to open us to the flow of the directions of spirit.

1. What are the things you do which displaces you from the center of happiness?

2. What should you do to place yourself in the center of happiness?

We consider the first divine enquiry and taught by the spirit of God, we realize the following:

You displace yourself from the center of happiness when:

- **You allow other people's attitudes to affect you**. This throws you out of balance. The being that God created in His image and likeness must cultivate attitudes that insulate them from other people's attitudes. People will always be what they are. People are continually acting out their past based on their conditionings. Most people intend good but they act on their limited knowledge, fears, and anger. The attitude you see is not about you; it is not meant to hurt you. You are not the target; it has deep-rooted causes.

- **You are overly concerned about people**. When your spirit of concern outstrips your spirit of management, there is confusion in you and you cannot effectively control your concern. If you do not see the solution for a problem, then realize that it is something for God to do. Simply put it on God's "to do" list and let go. Every invention was once a problem, so there is an inventive solution to the apparent problem.

To place ourselves in the center of happiness, you have to:

1. **Pray**. Many people consider prayer as the last option to their problems. That is an error. Prayer is the calling forth of your God magnificence into being. It is the doing of what God did in the beginning of creation when He said, "Let there be..." Each moment is the beginning of creation and yours is to call forth your goodness into manifestation. When you see the darkness thicken over the face of your world, it is time to say, "Let there be light. Let there be the light of my love, peace, understanding, etc." Prayer is a partnership with God.

2. **Meditate**. Meditation is to give attention to the virtues you are. When during the day, the world around you programs you to fear, anger, or suspicion, meditation will help you to recover from these false images forced upon you. You realize, *"I am the being that God created in His/Her image and likeness. I am the sound of goodness."* Meditation is a time to be friends with yourself, with who you truly are. Be still and give attention to the truth that you are divine, beautiful, healthy, and financially abundant. *For the earth is the Lord's and all its fullness.* You are one with God, so the earth and all its treasures are yours.

A Meditation Practice

This meditation ensures that the mind is focused on your essential nature. Meditation does not always have to be blank stillness. Many people cannot achieve this and their meditation periods can be wasted. The mind is used to being active and it is okay to keep it busy. The important thing is what it is busy with. In doing this process you may speak softly, hearing your voice in your solar plexus, or you may do the process mentally. In the process, notice the color and sound of your descriptions, along with their smell, taste, and feel.

Describe three central attitudes of yours which will ensure physiological, social, financial, psychological, and spiritual fulfillment, or identify one attitude that ensures you are balanced in all the [3]five regions of life. Give that attention now. Nothing that happens to you is for your misfortune. Whatever is happening in your life is growing you more into the image and likeness of God.

Step into this knowing: "I am here to be the highest good that life is seeking me to be." Whatever is happening in your life is calling forth the highest good that you are. Be still and give attention to the highest good you are here to be. Describe the attitude of this being that you are.

Thinking

Focus on and believe in the ideal world you know within. Do not conform to the world of bad news, statistics, and painful history. You knew this ideal world as a child; you lost it as you

---

[3] Man functions in five interconnected states, which are the physiological, social, psychological, financial, and spiritual.

conformed to the world of other people's vision. Be transformed by holding on to the internal vision.

1. Be a painter of what is possible and the world will look up to you.

2. You are not here to do it alone. You are supported by 5.98 sextillion metric tons (the weight of the earth) of power. With such a support you are immovable. You are supported and powered by the amount of force that spins the earth and moves it through space.

3. Have passion for your excellence and call it forth from every unit of life. Passion, I say, not compassion. See people as they are in their awesome magnificence and not as they present themselves as weak, incapacitated beings parading through life with their self pity, petty mediocrity, and box of woeful pictures of themselves, seeking compassion. You have no compassion to give. You are not asleep; you are conscious and you see through their masks. You see in each person the magnificent being that God created in His/Her spiritual image and likeness and your passion is to wake them up to it. So you do not have compassion for the weak, you have passion for their excellence.

Lessons on the Principle of the Quest for Happiness

1. Happiness does not happen automatically; you have to choose to make it happen and work at it.

2. Make yourself matter and be deserving of happiness.

3. When your concern spirit outstrips your management spirit, there is confusion in you and you cannot effectively help yourself.

4. If your happiness depends on external forces, you reduce yourself into a beggar.

5. To be unhappy for whatever reason is a mark of ingratitude and will certainly reduce you.

Benefits of Principle Sixteen

1. You are happy always, regardless of the circumstances you find yourself in.

2. You uplift and enrich the world.

3. You are healthy.

4. You enjoy your life and increase your passion for living.

PRINCIPLE 17
The Practice of Peace

Embrace your uniqueness.

Peace is the identification and free expression of your divine potential. Whatever you do that enhances your life in general is peace. What you do that enhances your physical life produces physiological peace or health. What enhances your relationships is social peace or harmony and for mental peace you experience tranquility. Spiritual peace is illumination; financial peace is riches and wealth. The various areas of your life blend to form the unique you and injury to any part of it hurts all parts of it.

Fear, anger, and negative emotions are the result of the loss of the sense of uniqueness. These negative emotions cause internal confusion that result in external conflict. They rob you of your creativity, destroy your confidence, and ruin your drive for excellence. It is fear and anger, for example, which cause most conflicts and war. To eradicate your negative emotions you must retrace yourself to your true identity.

As you became an adult, your desire to be accepted or to feel a sense of belonging coerced you to be something other than yourself. You thought this persona would be admired or accepted by others. In seeking to do things to please the group you belong to, you lost yourself. As a child, you were trying to shape yourself to satisfy the expectations of your parents and siblings. In adult life, you may have sought to meet the expected standards of your mate, teachers, or employers. In these pursuits, you ended up losing what you are that is truly you. Today, you are a mixture of many personalities. With these personalities you created your own labyrinth and lost your way in it.

Sometimes, it is worth emulating other people's attitudes and behaviors. However, you do not need to act like another person. You have to act like you, with your own uniqueness. Acting as you takes you out of negative competition and moves you from selfishness into self-wholeness. When you are lost to yourself, you are lost to peace. When you embody other people's personalities you are adulterating your persona and psyche and throwing yourself into self confusion. Existing fully for you takes away the drive to control and subjugate others. This results in peace with your environment.

There is no one like you and there never will be. Only you can do things the way you do. In your individuality are gifts that can enhance life. It is when you lose this individuality, trying to be something else, that you lose touch with your soul capabilities; and from that springs forth pain and evil.

A Practice for Peace

In seeking peace, men have devised all sorts of programs, but few address the need to be restored to their personal sense of uniqueness. It is no wonder that peace eludes man. To find peace, you need to retrace your steps to what you are and embrace your uniqueness.

Identify how you are different from your parents and all of the people you lived with while growing up. Watch your thoughts and identify the things you do and the thoughts you nurse which are the result of someone else's suggestions. Ask yourself, "What do I do like somebody else?" When you identify what you do like somebody else, ask yourself, "How do I do it like me or how do I choose to do it like me?" These inner probes and their responses will restore you to your own image and uniqueness. While growing up, a man heard his favorite aunt say, "I don't remember people's names." As an adult, his job will be greatly enhanced if he could remember people's names, but he couldn't. He stopped himself from remembering people's names and lost his free expression. When he was helped by this program, he let go of his aunt's image and stepped into his own and could remember names.

When you are truly you, you are god. You possess the peace that passes all human understanding. It is the peace that is there as you, uninfluenced by the presence of disease or health,; uninfluenced by the state of war and death or by a state of calm.

Lessons on the Principle of Peace

Peace is the identification and celebration of your uniqueness. All programs that do not address the restoration of personal uniqueness will not produce lasting peace.

Seeking to be like someone else is spiritual suicide; it negates you and causes internal confusion.

If you must emulate someone because of the person's good virtues, do so with your own uniqueness.

Benefits of Principle Seventeen

1. You enjoy your life and are peaceful.

2. You increase in the purity of your divine uniqueness.

You are happy, confident, creative, and responsible, and you have a drive for excellence.

PRINCIPLE 18

The Cosmic Intelligence at Work

Cooperate with the Purposeful Cosmic Intelligence that runs the universe for its highest good.

When I compiled this book, I was advised to make it universal by removing God from it. I did try but could not succeed. Everywhere I turn, Nature tells me of the absolute intelligence behind things.

You may have grown up in a religious home and always believed there is a God without questioning. Or you may be trying to rationalize the idea of God. Possibly, you have simply joined the masses in their God idea so you will not feel left out. Others are silenced because in the tradition in which they grew, it was taboo to consider such questions. You have the right to ask and know. How do our elders know there is God?

The answer is simple. If we can find intelligent happenings or events not caused by man, but upon which man depends, then that happening or event is caused by another power. Men call that power God. I choose to call it Cosmic, Love, Intelligence.

Our sole purpose in life is to give attention to the intention of this Intelligent Power. When you capture the intention of this Intelligence, that intention fertilizes your consciousness and manifests in your life as an individualized intelligence. The intention of this Intelligent Power is to amplify in you as your consciousness.

God realization is the alpha and omega of every spiritual quest. I invite you to God realization and celebration.

We shall cite a few examples that prove an intelligent power runs the universe so powerfully and perfectly that it does not require our input. There is an intelligent mind behind the washing machine, television, computer, and other marvels of science and technology. What intelligence is behind the rising sun? What intelligence is behind the seasons? Did it start with a big bang? If so, the Big Bang has infinite intelligence and purpose. That supreme intelligence and purpose is what men call God.

The cycle of night and day proves the existence of this intelligence. If the sun rises and does not set, life will perish. If it does not rise and it were to remain night, life will perish.

In the rising sun are life, energy, creativity, action, movement, and building energy. Plants grow their fruit in the dark. Each day, we grow shorter by about a quarter of an inch and are restored to our height in the night. In the darkness, therefore, are growth, rejuvenation, and restoration. For us to experience the alternating of rising sun and darkness, the earth has to spin on its axis at a speed of 1,000 mph. To get the changes in seasons that complements day and night for life to exist, it has to travel through space at a speed of 67,000 mph. Think of the force required to spin and move the earth for you to enjoy day and night and the changing seasons, all without the input of man. For an intelligent reason and purpose – that of sustaining life on earth – a huge force is spinning the earth and moving it through space. An Intelligent Presence must be behind it.

An intelligent power has designed that for life to be, the sun must rise, providing creativity, activity, motion, creation, food manufacturing, and sustenance. It has also designed that for life to exist, the darkness must "rise" to provide regeneration, rejuvenation, rest, renewal, and growth. All these happen without your input. If either of these were to prevail without the other, life on earth for man would perish.

The rising of your dark and light times are both necessary for your life to be. For your life on earth, many forces have been put in place. This tells you how important you are. Embrace your dark nights and your bright days equally. The universe is at congress for your highest good. All that happens to you is God. You realize, "Only God happens to me."

Again, when we look at the seasons, we realize that if one season were to prevail for all time, life would perish. One season following another is necessary for the sustenance of life. The change of seasons is essential for the maintenance of life, and seeing this you realize that the changes in your life are for the maintenance of your life.

We see intelligence in atoms that determines how they bond with other atoms to form molecules. Now think of other purposeful happenings in life and provide your own proof that some Intelligent Being is behind them. With the immense intelligence we see in life, we conclude that God, the absolute intelligence, is present in and as all of life.

African mystics do not only believe in a transcendental God. They believe also in a personal God who is evident in all life forms. God can be touched, seen with the naked eyes, and experienced with all the senses. It is for this reason that the African mystic teaches that "no one teaches God to a child." The means that God is self-evident and does not need teaching. God must be an individual personal experience but God is so self-evident that Its discovery is not a task but simply calls for a little contemplation. So we contemplate God to discover Its presence and fertilize our consciousness with It.

To seek only a transcendental experience of God is like taking alcohol to forget your sorrows. When the alcohol clears, you are back to the pain. God is immanent as well as transcendental.

Cosmic Intelligence Is Self Supporting

The one Life is expressed as the life of each of the elements such that life will perish if any of the elements were missing. For example, there would be no life without any one of the elements of air or fire, water or earth. Each is full of life but the life of each is supported by the life of the other. Here we see a purposeful, self-supporting law at work; it demands of each element to support the others.

Just as each element is so important that without it life would perish, so it is that you are so important that without you life will perish. The life you live is part of the one life and is indestructible. So you step into the knowing that you are indestructible. You may change your body garments, but the life you live is indestructible. Think of how the act of respiration contracts and expands the stomach, assisting it to digest food and extract nutrients for the body. Think of your rhythmic heartbeat that handles your circulatory system, all without your input. If things were to happen by chance, the eyes of many people might be found on their feet! Think of what a problem that would be. Again, we see a self-supporting order as the nature of Cosmic Intelligence.

In a papaya, we capture the intention of Cosmic Intelligence to infinitely increase and multiply Itself. We see in the fruit the power of self-sustenance and self-expansion. In the papaya, the intelligence is inherent to make this happen. We realize that the intelligence to sustain and maintain itself is within the body of the universe and in all of nature. So you step into the realization that "in me is the inherent intelligence of the universe for my self-maintenance and expansion." This awareness does not flow as a mere affirmation but as a word of power from a place of pure knowing. It is not an affirmation; it is a declaration of Nature's truth. Your realization of Cosmic Intelligence in the things of nature builds your faith and becomes for you the basis or building blocks of things not yet seen in their physical form. You live from a place of exhaustless knowing that nourishes everything you do.

When you understand that an intelligent power runs the entire universe, you begin to study it and cooperate with it. The frustration of many people is due to their not understanding the plan, purpose, and direction of life as a whole. Thus, they sometimes fight against the current of life and experience pain. When you understand the Cosmic Intelligence Principle, you are at peace with yourself.

What we call calamities is often the way life is recreating or regenerating itself. Storms at sea are the processes of life mixing oxygen into the water for marine life nourishment. Earthquakes are the means of life creating more fertile soil. Floods are another means of life creating fertile lands. There is meaningful purpose for all happenings.

Just as the air surrenders to you for your sustenance, your body eventually will nourish other life forms. But your body is not the real you. The real you is spirit and eternal. Everyone exits the body by some means or another; when your time to exit the body comes, surrender it joyfully.

Trust and Faith in God

Trust Life! Trust the Cosmic Intelligence. The world came to a standstill when Princess Diana of Great Britain died. But the volume of tears and sorrow could not stop the grave from accepting her mortal remains. In all of this, few people stopped to ask what great purpose her life fulfilled. The purposeful order cannot wait on human understanding; whatever is happening fits into a larger plan.

From our contemplation we see an infinitely loving presence, pure purposefulness, and an endless intelligence that runs the universe, such that another power cannot exist. We see life or Cosmic Intelligence as truly omnipresent, graciously filling everything with abundance. We realize in contemplation that we are expressions of Cosmic Intelligence and we bring this awareness into manifestation as our experience.

I know that you are awakened to a power operating abundantly within and around you in perfect precision and that your life is blessed. Life is full of opposites and multiplicity that complement each other. You embrace the opposites, the duality, and you see the unity in duality and in multiplicity. You are thus in a place of wholeness and power, supported by the infinite intelligence that runs, maintains, sustains, and recreates itself as the universe. There is peace and progress in your world now and always.

Scripture says that you are created in the spiritual image and likeness of this awesome intelligence. "How magnificent you are as the being that Cosmic Intelligence created in His or Her spiritual image and likeness!"

Pause and contemplate that statement now. Be filled with the wonderment and intelligence happening in your own body. Through your body you touch God.

A closer embrace of Cosmic Intelligence is all you need. What will you be with all of the powers of Cosmic Intelligence activated in you? Is that a possibility? The answer is yes, and many of us are on that road.

The secret is this: you manifest the evidence of Cosmic Intelligence you see in your life. To heal a wound or to accelerate such healing, I ask the seeker to contemplate how the bark of a tree grows back when you cut it. An intelligent power within the tree knows that it must heal itself and knows how to bring this about. By focusing on and contemplating this, you activate that healing power in your own consciousness and thus experience your own healing. It is that simple. Find the evidence of Cosmic Intelligence in the life around you and the same evidence will manifest in your life. This is what we call "The Direct Path to Power Transformation." God, the Cosmic Intelligence, is an infinite marvel to be explored and experienced. The more you explore and prove Its existence by clear evidence to your consciousness, the more Godlike and God-aware you become.

In African Healing practice from ancient to present time, focusing on the evidence of God is a powerful healing practice. Traditional healers heal broken bones with this procedure. For example, a man with a broken leg is treated in this way: the practitioner takes hold of a cock or hen according to the gender of the patient. He breaks the leg of the bird to correspond to the broken leg of the patient. He does this in the presence of the patient so that the bird cannot walk just as the patient cannot. The leg of the bird as well as the patient is reset and bandaged with herbs. The bird is allowed to walk freely, but within the environment of the patient. The patient is to focus on the bird and with this comes fast recovery. Within a fortnight, the leg of the bird heals completely and so does the patient's leg.

The healing secret is that, in addition to the herbs used, the patient's mind is focused on the evidence of healing taking place in the bird. His or her consciousness is then fertilized by the rapid healing development of the bird. This expedites his or her healing. For whatever difficulty you go through a corresponding healing evidence of Cosmic Intelligence is available in nature. By identifying it you embody it and you have your healing solution to the difficulty.

If you can prove the power of Cosmic Intelligence to your mind, that power becomes your power. Spirit has all power but this power is revealed to you and through you as you become conscious of it. Contemplate a manifesting power of Cosmic Intelligence and embody it.

The more evidence of Cosmic Intelligence you find, the more evidences of Cosmic Intelligence present themselves in your life and the more your joy, love, and power increase.

When you mention the word God, it is no more just a word; it is power, love, joy, and creativity. The practice of God awareness is the secret of healing and of every achievement. You pray from the place where your consciousness is bursting and vibrating with the energy of Cosmic Intelligence.

What the Cosmic Intelligence Is Not

If you have been presented with some bad pictures of a god created after human concepts and selfishness, you need to heal those pictures now.

Three quarters of the wars in the world are fought in the name of God. The idea of people fighting for God is ridiculous because it presupposes that God has no power to fight for himself. Ninety-nine percent of the conflicts in the human soul are the result of having some false concept about God. An internal war is going on in the souls of men. People put words into the mouth of God and use them to oppress others. We are presented with a god who gets angry, hates, and puts people into burning fire. These pictures of God instill fear. A true healing must present the true God.

Can God hate, get angry, and be destructive? How would you feel towards such a god? Even an earthly mother, knowing her son committed a murder, would not allow him to be sentenced to death. She would plead for mercy. God, who is the absolute wisdom of the universe, has infinitely more love and mercy.

Let's reason this way: if you had the wisdom and intelligence of every man on the planet, would you be offended by anything anyone does? The answer is no. Would God, the absolute wisdom of the universe, get offended at your errors? Take a look at yourself; you may laugh at some of the wrong things you did as a child. If even you laugh at your past errors, would any of those errors offend God so much that he would put you in hell? Almost everyone is one way or the other affected by this kind of religious abuse and you need to heal these fearful pictures of God. Probably, these erroneous teachings were given with the good intention of keeping men under control and from willingly doing wrong. If it were so, we no more need such fearful pictures of Cosmic, Love, Intelligence to keep us from doing wrong. We need to understand spiritual law to keep us from doing wrong.

The following references are Bible related but the same pictures of God are present in most of the traditional religions.

1. A god who hates, gets angry, and is destructive cannot be a true God. Such a god needs a therapist.

2. Would you test your child when you know your child will fail and when he has failed would you curse him? Of course not and God knows better.

3. That cannot be a true god who created man and put him in the garden with a [4]temptation he knew his creation would fail and when failing, curse them.

4. That cannot be a true god who harbors [5]regrets for creating man. To regret is to acknowledge failure. Cosmic, Love, Intelligence cannot fail.

5. That cannot be a true god who instructs one tribe/race to go and [6]kill another tribe/race utterly.

6. That cannot be a true god who, after creating man in his spiritual image and likeness, cursed him. Did God curse his own spiritual self that is manifested as man? He must be a self-accursed god to curse his own spiritual image and likeness.

7. That cannot be a true god who prefers one sex (the male sex) over another sex. That cannot be a true god who [7]accepts people of one creed and rejects all others, who for no fault of theirs were born into other belief systems.

---

[4] Genesis 2:16. God told man not to eat of the tree of the knowledge of good and evil He has placed in the Garden of Eden.

[5] Genesis 6:7. God repented that he created man.

[6] 1 Samuel 15:18. God commanded the destruction of the Amalekites.

[7] The traditional religious bodies believe and teach that those who do not belong to their faith are not accepted of God and will be roasted in hell fire.

8. That cannot be a true god who was [8]outwitted in heaven by his arch-rival, the devil, and the devil succeeded in staging a coup in heaven.

9. That cannot be a true god who, as recorded in Revelations, needed help, from the angel Michael, to fight the devil when he staged a coup in heaven.

10. That cannot be a true god who when he failed to destroy the devil, cast him down on earth to haunt his creation and ordained hell for all who follow this devil, who could outwit even him, god.

11. That cannot be a true god who to pacify his weak conscience for sending the devil here to plague men, sent his son to spill his blood as a means of [9]reconciliation with his creation. How can a true god need reconciliation?

The questions are endless.

The Vast Nature of God

God must be and is infinitely loving, endlessly intelligent, and truly all-powerful, such that another power cannot exist besides him in an everlasting war; He/She must be and is truly omnipresent, filling everything and abundantly gracious. There

---

[8] Revelation 12:7-11. There was mutiny in heaven. When God realized it, He and his angels led by the angel Michael fought the devil. The devil was not destroyed but was cast down to the earth.

[9] Romans 5:10. Through the death of Jesus, the son of God, we are reconciled unto God.

is nothing to fear or run away from, because [10]even if you make your bed in hell, that is, if it exists at all, you will be embraced by the loving presence of God. This realization lifts you above common thinking. Take a look and you will realize that all common thinking is fear based. The nuclear bombs are built as a result of fear of one nation for another. Lifted above common thinking your thoughts are free, creative, and healing. You simply embody your true glorious self, which was present with the Father/Mother God before the worlds were formed. Yours is Peace and Love in your soul always. "And So It Is."

Until we read the Bible and other religious books as spiritual books and not as storybooks, and think through the allegories of those books to find their spiritual import, we capture a god created after the likeness of the fear and confusion of man.

The mental pictures we have about God do not produce love for God. "Loving God with all your heart and with all your might and your neighbor as yourself" is impossible to do for a fickle-minded, scary, wicked, psychopathic god.

The pictures of God as taught by traditional religions produce fear and doubt. The verse II Timothy 1:7 states that the true God has not given us the spirit of fear and timidity but of love, power and a sound mind. Fear attracts into your consciousness the object you fear. At the same time it repels you from God.

---

[10] Psalm 139: 7-10. Where can I go from your Spirit? Where can I flee from your presence? If I go up to the heavens, you are there; if I make my bed in the depths (hell), you are there. If I rise on the wings of the dawn, if I settle on the far side of the sea, even there your hand will guide me, your right hand will hold me fast.

You attract the fearful graven images of God as your experience and this distances you from God.

Popular belief is not necessarily right – Be not [11]conformed to this world and its ideas but be ye transformed by the renewal of your mind.

Contemplate on your own mother and father's intention or prayer for you. You can feel what your mother's prayer for you would be. It would be full of expectations of unqualified greatness. With all of the errors of your parents, they envision greatness for you. What will you be if you were to embody all the prayers of your parents? Similarly, you can embody the intention of the universe for you. The universe is the body of God. What God intends or prays for you must happen. You awaken to the realization that you are the answer to the prayer of Father/Mother God. To the question of what is God, we discover that…

God is the intelligence within the hydrogen atom that knows that two of itself must come together with an oxygen atom to form a water molecule.

God is the ever-present intelligence within the cell that knows how to produce protein, carry it throughout the body, breathe, and regenerate.

God is the ever-present intelligence within the hundred billion cells that form the human body, with specialized systems known as organs. Cells in one organ are different from the cells in another, and God is the ever-present intelligence within each cell that makes it know where it belongs. God is the ever-

---

[11] Romans 12:2

present intelligence within the organs that makes them know how to relate with one another, all without our human intervention.

There are over a thousand species of fishes and birds with varying shades of colors. The master artist and designer responsible for this beauty is God.

There are over six and half billion people on this planet alone, all with different features and thumbprints.

God is the ever-present intelligence creating this beauty, this wonderment. What of the wonderment in the animal and vegetable kingdoms? The marvel is infinite. To be conscious of this is to be in harmony with the true miracle of your being.

The earth with its entire marvel is but a drop of water in the ocean, when compared to the solar system that contains it and God is the ever-present intelligence within the solar system.

The solar system is but a drop of water in the ocean when compared to the Milky Way galaxy within which the solar system is contained. To talk about God is to talk about the awesome indwelling presence, so awesome that we are truly humbled. Science, today, has discovered a hundred billion galaxies so spread apart that the Milky Way galaxy is but an atom in the ocean when compared to the discovered universe and God is the ever-present intelligence within the universe. Truly, there is no other God but Allah. This universe is a miracle and to be conscious of it is to be in harmony with an ever-happening miracle. Meditating on this daily is to tune yourself to the miracle that God is as you.

Man the Summation or Miniature of Cosmic Intelligence

"Let us create man in our own image and likeness." That is the summation of the universes of intelligence of God replicating itself as man. And God blessed you to be fruitful, and to multiply and replenish the earth and subdue it. That makes five blessings. You are the five times blessed spiritual child of God.

- The earth is 75% water and the human body is likewise.
- The moon goes around the earth in 28 days and so do women have their menses every 28 days.
- The moon causes the sea to have high and low tides and so are men influenced.

We see that the same principle of law and order that governs the universe runs the life of all men and life forms on earth. When we understand this Cosmic, Love, Intelligence and cooperate with it, we have endless days of bliss.

Such is the God who created you in His/Her spiritual image and likeness, and endowed you with a creative nature so you can create your world freely. Whatever you choose to create is your instant possession and experience.

You are a spirit being having a human experience. Rise now into the consciousness of God and know that you cannot have a separate existence from God and where the spirit of the Lord is there is liberty. Scripture says that God has not given us the spirit of fear, but of love, power and of a sound mind. Whatever inspires fear in you is not of God.

Choose this day what you will serve; the pseudo gods the world created in order to control, dominate and manipulate you, or the living, true Omnipotent, Omnipresent and Omniscient God that has sustained and maintained the whole universe since the first day His words went forth into creation.

For the vastness and the infinite intelligence of what God is, many things purported to have been said or done by Him could not be possible.

The Practice of Conscious Oneness with Cosmic Intelligence

1. Allow your eyes to close and make this enquiry several times to yourself, responding with a vivid description of what you are. *When God is God as me, what am I (like)?* You may substitute this statement with any that inspired you when you read through this principle. As you progress in your response, change the enquiry to *Now that God is God as me, what am I (like)?*

2. As you make this statement listen to your life and notice what past events it is addressing. Notice the times you may have thought of yourself as being less than divine perfection.

3. When you find an event that this statement is addressing, locate yourself at the beginning of that event. To be sure that you are in that event, notice what you are seeing, hearing, tasting, smelling, and feeling. While in that event, describe yourself several times. Look into the face of the person involved, if any, and make the statement.

4. Repeat steps one to three several times, allowing it to address other cuds or to stimulate abilities.

5. End your session by allowing your eyes to open.

Lessons on the Principle of God

1. There is an awesome Cosmic, Love Intelligence that runs the universe. It operates within the universe as the body of the universe. Some call it God. It is called by other names in other languages. The lily or the jasmine will give off their fragrance if you were to call them by any other name because it is their nature to fulfill themselves by giving off fragrance. Similarly, God is God, no matter what name you use.

2. God cannot burden or sabotage itself by creating an opposing power within its own field of existence. Every life form supports some other life form so we know from this that the nature of God is self-supporting of itself and not sabotaging itself.

3. Cosmic Intelligence works for your good because by its nature and law it can only work for its own good.

4. Cosmic Intelligence has infinite pointers to its existence. You need to prove its existence to yourself and doing so opens you up to the power.

5. Trust in the Cosmic Intelligence absolutely.

Benefits of Principle Eighteen

1. You are at one and at peace with God, the Cosmic Intelligence.

2. You understand the principle of law and order that runs the universe and you cooperate with it for harmony and healing.

3. You express as the field of possibilities.

Appendix

Release Program One

1. Read through the principle and analyze its meaning and importance to your life. The principle will inspire wisdom to clear a painful issue or activate an unused ability in your life.

2. Notice what the principle is addressing in your past, present, and future life.

3. Write the inspiration sentence(s) that came to you and that addresses specific issues in your life. This sentence is your Healing Message or Release Statement.

4. Allow your eyes to close and state the Healing Message several times. Pause between statements to assimilate the full import of the healing message. Notice the smell, taste, feel, sound, and color of the healing message.

5. Take a breath and allow that breath to take you to the issue in your past, present, or future that it is to address. Locate yourself in that issue and minister the Healing Message to it. You minister by stating the Healing Message to the event or issue. Do this several times until you feel the release or the activation of ability.

6. When you are done, take another breath and let it bring you to present time; then allow your eyes to open.

Repeat steps 4 – 6 for all the healing messages you found in step three.

To get your life healing messages, use the following probes or create similar ones.

1. How is this Principle addressing my financial life?
2. How is this Principle addressing my social life?
3. How is this Principle addressing my spiritual life?
4. How is this Principle addressing my physiological life?
5. How is this Principle addressing my psychological life?
6. How is this Principle addressing my personal life?
7. How is this Principle addressing my sex life?
8. How is this Principle addressing my family life?
9. How is this Principle addressing my relationship with my church or club?
10. How is this Principle addressing my relationship with my nation?
11. How is this Principle addressing my relationship with my world of all races?
12. What in this Principle is for the empowerment of my financial life?
13. What in this Principle is for the empowerment of my social life?

14. What in this Principle is for the empowerment of my spiritual life?

15. What in this Principle is for the empowerment of my physiological life?

16. What in this Principle is for the empowerment of my psychological life?

17. What in this Principle is for the empowerment of my personal life?

18. What in this Principle is for the empowerment of my sex life?

19. What in this Principle is for the empowerment of my family life?

20. What in this Principle is for the empowerment of my church or club?

21. What in this Principle is for the empowerment of my nation?

22. What in this Principle is for the empowerment of my world of all races?

Release Program Two

Discovering Life Lessons and Capturing Soul God Messages to Address Your Life

1. Read each of the principles in this book.

2. Capture three or more lessons you got from each one which you feel addresses a part of your life. We call these Life Lessons and they are seeking to address a portion of your life. They are either to address a pain in your life that needs cleansing or an inner potential that needs activation, reinforcement and/or expansion.

3. Capture three or more lessons or inspirations that flashed or dawned on you as you read but which were not from what you read. These are your Soul Messages addressing portions of your life. These sudden flashes or realization came to you because something in you, seeking healing, led you to capture those lessons so you can use them for healing. These Soul Messages always reveal the pain that needs to be addressed but is often ignored. In staying only with the moment's good feelings, you miss the transformation called for. This Soul Message is valuable because it carries with it the energy to quickly erase the energy in that past painful event so it can no longer be triggered to control you. This is an easy and powerful way to process yourself daily. A Soul Message may also address an inner potential that needs activation, reinforcement and expansion.

4. Return in your mind to the time the event that holds the pain took place. Let the Life Lessons (lessons you got

from the principle) as well as your Soul Messages in step 2 and 3 above respectively, minister to the pain picture to bring out the learning it was meant to give you at the time it happened so healing can take place. *"As a result of the Life Lessons and Soul Messages, what does the pain mean to you?"* The pain and its root cause do not dissolve when you use only the Present Time lesson and move forward. You must use the Past Time lesson and handle the pain as a present tense happening. To return to an event is to recall the Time, Energy, Space, and Circumstance in which it occurred. For example, identify what you were seeing, hearing, tasting, smelling and feeling in that event.

5. The next thing is to trace the earliest pain event similar to this. Bring it to the center of your mind and let the Life Lessons (lessons you got from the principle) as well as your Soul Messages in (b) and (c) above respectively minister to it to bring out the learning it was meant to give you at the time it happened so healing can take place. Do the same for all the similar events to Present Time.

If these Life Lessons and Soul Messages stimulated a positive emotion, go through the same procedure to empower and enlarge your spiritual assets. The creative or happy event is your Christ asset and needs to be nursed and enlarged. Ask yourself, "In what ways can this good be repeated or expanded to bless others?"

Release Program Three

In each incarnation, life gives you the full opportunity to attain spiritual freedom, or salvation as it is called in Christianity. The voice of spirit has always been with you to show you how but unfortunately many do not heed or do not know how to heed.

A serious healing program is required for the soul to be free since it carries some cuds from many past lives. Provided here are five separate healing programs, using Soul Processing.

1. Prepare a salvation notebook. This book contains events in which life was a pleasant celebration for you. When in pain read a message in your salvation notebook and make decisions from the place of joy. Determine the outcome of your pain from a place of joy.

    a) You may also step into other people's victories, embody them as yours and use them to run fresh outcome until you feel it happening and done. *"The one life that Jesus is, is my life. I embody the victory of Jesus' forgiving spirit filled with omniscient wisdom. In this wisdom, I rejoice at the inner freedom that I feel and the great joy that this event brings to all who share my life in various ways. I am thankful."*

2. Painful things are bound to happen but you are entitled to a positive outcome of bad events. Bless and embrace present and past pains with the determined outcome. Step into a past pain and with will/decision, state your determined outcome in the midst of the pain.

3. When in pain, be on your guard and watch statements coming from sympathizers. Translate them instantly to reflect your determined outcome.

4. Be on your guard when you have to sympathize with someone in pain, or else you may borrow and embody the person's pain. Bring the person's mind into the good that is seeking to emerge out of their situation.

5. Discovering Life Lessons and capturing Soul God Messages to address your life:

   a) Read a Principle in this book.

   b) Capture three or more lessons that you got out from it which you felt addressed a part of your life. We call these Life Lessons and they are seeking to address a portion of your life. Use the chart below to record them.

   c) Capture three or more lessons or inspirations that flashed on your mind which were not from what you read. These are your God Soul Messages addressing portions of your life. These sudden flashes or realizations came to you because portions of you, seeking healing, led you to capture those lessons so you can use them for healing. These God Soul Messages always reveal to you the pain that needs healing but you often ignore both the lessons and the pains they are to address. You stay only with the moment's good feelings and thus miss the transformation called for. These God messages are valuable because they carries the energy to quickly erase the energy in past painful events so they can no longer be triggered to control you. This is the easiest way to process yourself daily. It is the best and most advanced Soul Processing.

d) Return in your mind to the time the event that holds the pain took place. Let the Life Lessons as well as your God Soul Messages in (b) and (c) above respectively, minister to the pain pictures to bring out the learning they were meant to give you at the time the painful events happened in order for healing to take place. *"As a result of the Life Lessons or God Soul Messages, what does the pain mean to you?"* The pain and its root cause do not dissolve when you use the lesson in the Present Time and move forward. You must take the lessons to the past and handle the pain as a present tense happening. To return to an event is to recall the Time, Energy, Space, and Circumstance in which it occurred. When is it happening, who do you see, what do you hear?

e) The next thing is to trace the earliest pain event similar to this. Bring it to the center of your mind and let the Life Lessons as well as your God Soul Messages in (b) and (c) above respectively minister to it to bring out the learning it was meant to give you at the time it happened in order for healing to take place. Do the same for all the similar events to Present Time.

f) The Life Lessons and God Soul Messages may also stimulate a positive emotion relating to a pleasant event. In this case, it is requesting you to reinforce or enlarge an ability of your soul. Go through the same procedure to empower and enlarge your spiritual asset. The creative or happy event is your Christ

g) asset and needs to be nursed and enlarged. Your inner prompt is, *"In what ways can this good be repeated or be made to bless others?"*

You can combine programs one and five for a master soul cleansing and empowerment. Allow the teachings to process your past limitations. Freed from the past, you can enjoy the present and move successfully into the future.

Healing My Life

Use the following samples to chart out your areas of spiritual growth

Lessons From The Teaching/Reading	Areas Of My Life It Addresses	Period In My Life In Which I Need This Lesson
Trust the process of life.	1. The fear that my children will leave me when they are grown. 2. The fear of old age.	1. 1984, when my mother died. 2. 1977, my father was a vegetable when he died.

Inspirations From The Teaching/Reading	Areas Of My Life It Addresses	Period In My Life In Which I Need This Lesson
Most things we fear never happen, but they cause us disease.	I feared my son would die as a result of the car accident.	1990, In London.

The Way Forward

You have eighteen routes to the center of fulfilled living. What is most important is to use these principles to fully cleanse your life from all of the injurious beliefs you may have already filed in your consciousness. Use these principles also to reinforce the life-enhancing wisdom you may have grown with.

Beyond the principles are the well-chartered workshops for soul cleansing and empowerment. Each principle is also well discussed on Video and Audio Compact Disks. They are a great resource for understanding the principles and their practice. These are available to you from our center.

I welcome you to greater growth.

Brother Ishmael Tetteh

Conscious Humanity, Inc.
1632 Rodney Drive
Los Angeles, California 90027
Tel: 760 633 1033
Email: conscioushumanity@gmail.com
Web Site: www.conscioushumanity.com